Little things change
everything !

Jon Gordon

Praise for *Positive Chaos*

"*Positive Chaos* is an extraordinary contribution and must-read for the turbulent times we're experiencing. Get this book for all your leaders, and those who are stuck in limiting patterns."

DR. NIDO R. QUBEIN, president of High Point University and Horatio Alger Award recipient

"*Positive Chaos* helped me shift my mindset to see crisis and chaos from a whole new perspective. It's a great read that provided me with practical tools to put chaos to work!"

PATRICK APPLEBY, president of WinnResidential

"This book will forever change how you perceive and respond to chaos at work and in life. If you feel overwhelmed, stressed out, and powerless, read *Positive Chaos* to see the patterns and seize opportunities all around you!"

LT. COL. WALDO WALDMAN, *New York Times*– and *Wall Street Journal*–bestselling author of *Never Fly Solo*

"A prescriptive and relevant road map to creating positive direction, safety, and true stability in an ever-changing and chaotic world."

CLINT PULVER, author of *I Love It Here*

"*Positive Chaos* is the map you need to find true success and happiness in today's crazy, turbulent, overwhelming world. Dan Thurmon shows you how to take back control of your life. Highly recommended!"

JAY BAER, bestselling author of *Hug Your Haters*

"*Positive Chaos* helps you use what's 'out of control' to fuel your future, life, and leadership."

PHIL M. JONES, bestselling author of *Exactly What to Say*

"*Positive Chaos* is distinctive. Dan Thurmon not only highlights the turmoil many of us feel, but he also delivers meaningful and detailed specifics on developing the skill set required to thrive among today's disorder and the anxiety it can bring."

SCOTT MCKAIN, author of *ICONIC*

"Dan Thurmon always delivers. *Positive Chaos* is an off-the-charts must-read for leaders, or anyone who wants to break through old patterns and reach new levels of personal growth and success."

VANESSA FUKUNAGA, president/CEO of Engel & Völkers Snell Real Estate and CEO/publisher of Ocean Blue World

"Through groundbreaking research, insightful examples, and powerful stories, Dan Thurmon challenges our thinking and invites us to reset our expectations. *Positive Chaos* will have you reexamining your present in order to create a compelling future."

SKIP PRICHARD, CEO of OCLC, Inc. and *Wall Street Journal*–bestselling author of *The Book of Mistakes*

"I'm buying this book for my entire team! *Positive Chaos* is a unique and profound work for the times. It's changed the way I conceptualize chaos, and I'm now more capable and confident than ever before."

DANI STERN, COO of Blue Water Development Company

"Believe it or not, chaos can be a good thing. In *Positive Chaos*, Dan Thurmon helps you understand today's chaos, simplify the complex, and take confident steps forward!"

SHEP HYKEN, *New York Times*–bestselling author of *The Amazement Revolution*

POSITIVE
CHAOS

POSITIVE

DAN THURMON

CHAOS

Transform Crisis into Clarity and Advantage

PAGE TWO

Cataloguing in publication information is
available from Library and Archives Canada.
ISBN 978-1-77458-288-6 (hardcover)
ISBN 978-1-77458-289-3 (ebook)

Page Two
pagetwo.com

Edited by Sarah Brohman
Copyedited by Rachel Ironstone
Proofread by Alison Strobel
Jacket design by Cameron McKague
Interior design and illustrations by Taysia Louie
Indexed by Donald Howes
Printed and bound in Canada by Friesens
Distributed in Canada by Raincoast Books
Distributed in the US and internationally by Macmillan

23 24 25 26 27   5 4 3 2 1

danthurmon.com

To Shay, my wife,
my stability in chaos, and
the complexity I choose.

CONTENTS

FOREWORD

WHEN DAN THURMON asked me to write the foreword to his new book, the one you have just started reading, I felt greatly honored and said yes immediately. After reading the manuscript, cover to cover, I was even more excited, as it is a remarkable work, filled with both the origins and latest research on chaos coupled with stories, interviews, specific insights, and actionable strategies for both individuals and organizations. Dan delivers on the promise the title of this book makes to you, the reader.

I know the importance of writing a book that can touch a reader deeply, as a *New York Times-*, *Wall Street Journal-*, and Amazon-bestselling author who has written seven books that are in dozens of languages. I share this not to brag, but instead to let you know that I know what makes a good book great, and *this* is a great book.

Dan is the perfect author for a book about Positive Chaos, as he embodies this philosophy and the principles he teaches in his own life every single day. In his speeches, with his consulting and coaching clients, and during his time as the president of the National Speakers Association, I have watched Dan develop a powerful methodology to transform chaos from a debilitating force into a powerful advantage. Because Dan and I are in a mastermind group together, I know the amount of research and effort he has put into this book. On a personal level, I can share with you that Dan always gives his all to whatever he sets out to do. For that reason, he has the highest respect of his professional colleagues, and as you read this book, you will be the recipient of all his wisdom, time, and effort.

Dan has a passion for helping people. It's just part of his DNA! And as a highly successful entrepreneur, consultant, author, and keynote speaker, he knows how to use great storytelling filled with examples to bring his key points to life.

Why This Book Is So Important Now!

Let's face it, chaos can strike anytime, anyplace, and in many ways. For example, when the stock market takes a major dive, that can trigger financial chaos. When major layoffs are announced with little additional information, work chaos can erupt. When a thunderstorm shuts down an entire airport, travel chaos quickly follows. When a spouse says they are leaving the marriage, relationship chaos often follows. And when, heaven forbid, someone gets a very bad diagnosis, health-related chaos quickly follows.

In all these examples, everything was normal, predictable, and safely moving at a manageable pace—that is, until something seemingly out of the blue happened, usually occurring fast, that created chaos.

You have personally experienced chaos many times, and in many ways, during your life. And as a professional futurist and disruptive innovation expert, I can easily predict that you will experience chaos many more times in the future. The amount of chaos, and the level of chaos, will dramatically accelerate over time; I call this a *future fact* because it will happen.

Why am I so confident in calling this a future fact? If we just look at technology-driven exponential change, it has been accelerating for quite some time now. And as you know, exponential change starts out slow but accelerates increasingly over time. When the global pandemic erupted in March of 2020, people and organizations were forced to change, sending many into chaos. Streets around the world were empty and many businesses shut down because we didn't know much about this new virus except that it was airborne, highly contagious, and deadly. The result: we all went digital at an amazing new level—shopping online, working from home, and having countless virtual meetings. We started talking to our doctors using our computer, and teachers learned to educate students through the screen. The list of chaotic disruptions could go on for pages.

Over twenty-five technology categories, including cloud computing and artificial intelligence, accelerated ten years in less than twelve months. In other words, technology-driven change accelerated at a pace beyond exponential levels. And this in turn created both chaos and beyond exponential *opportunities* for those who understood how to find opportunities in chaos, as Dan is teaching you in this book.

We have now entered a period of technology-enabled transformation that is moving ever faster. The good news is that *Positive Chaos* teaches you how to take advantage of all this, and the principles can help you elevate how you deal with accelerating change while you engage with transformation in new and powerful ways.

As a technology futurist with a forty-year track record of accurate predictions in my newsletters, articles, books, and the over three thousand keynote speeches I have given around the world, I can easily state that the prediction above regarding more chaos ahead is a future fact.

To thrive in the years and decades ahead, *Positive Chaos* will arm you with practical, actionable strategies you can apply to both your personal and business life to transform crisis into clarity and advantage and to thrive in the years and decades ahead. Enjoy!

DANIEL BURRUS
Bestselling author of seven books, including *Technotrends*, *Flash Foresight*, and *The Anticipatory Organization*

INTRODUCTION
THE TRUTH ABOUT CHAOS

---

79 percent of working Americans believe a crisis of constant, ever-increasing chaos exists in America.

Impact of Chaos in the American Workforce study

"CHANGE MANAGEMENT" used to be simpler. You could take your time contemplating what's coming, evaluating the evolving landscape of your life and business. You could build graphs and pie charts of the factors influencing change and carefully weigh the pros and cons of available options. Then, with sufficient data and the support of others, you could confidently act and implement your three-year plan.

Today, however, the idea of relying on a three-year plan seems ridiculous. Waves of change are steadily increasing in both size and frequency. The potential impact and devastation seem enormous. Just when you've wrapped your mind around one factor, you see another, larger swell headed your way. All the while, you wonder what you *don't* see and are anxious about how that will disrupt your life—again.

This is chaos. But chaos isn't one thing. It feels like *everything*, all at once.

For example, the COVID-19 pandemic changed everything in some ways and many things in huge ways. Some aspects of life and business are forever altered. Additionally, we face monumental, accelerated changes to the economy, cost of living, culture, supply chains, energy demands, and governmental regulations; the rise of digital currencies and Web 3.0 and 4.0; and, of course, omnipresent social media, artificial intelligence, and political divisions, all of which fuel our fear and anxiety.

When the statistic that opens this introduction surfaced in our study, it stopped me in my tracks. Think about it. Almost 80 percent of working Americans believe we are in a crisis of relentless chaos that is constantly increasing and intensifying. Many also believe chaos is causing personal and professional harm to them, while also limiting their opportunities and happiness. As perception creates reality, this shared belief results in various versions of a similar experience.

Obviously, *this* common experience of reality isn't enjoyable. In fact, it sucks! Specifically, it sucks energy, purpose, confidence, creativity, and human connection. Instead of bringing out your best, most beneficial, and encouraging characteristics, this perceived chaos keeps you in "survival mode." While experiencing the combined conditions it creates, it is far more difficult to lead others or build a business. More importantly, perhaps, you can't fully experience joy and happiness, meaningful purpose, and deep love. In a state of perpetual urgency, distraction, and trepidation, you won't be able to effectively lead a family or build a satisfying life.

I'll also tell you what you already know on some level: this condition is not sustainable. When you race against life, or simply apply your personal will and effort against the forces of chaos, you may manage for a time. Eventually, however, you'll crumble and collapse because disruption never tires. Chaos never rests. We feel its ominous presence all around us. But what is chaos, exactly?

In our groundbreaking *Impact of Chaos in the American Workforce* study, before we presented the specific definition and context, we asked one thousand participants to answer the open-ended question, "How would you define chaos?" Their answers included:

"Confusion because everything is happening at once."

"Total absence of order or structure."

"The world we live in right now."

"Unmanageable stress that is out of control."

"My marriage."

The list went on with other variations. They were almost all negative, fearful, and deeply personal. How would *you* define chaos?

The *Oxford Languages* online dictionary defines *chaos* like this:

chaos (noun)

1a: Complete disorder and confusion.

1b: Behavior so unpredictable as to appear random, owing to great sensitivity to small changes in conditions.

As you contemplate this definition, does it resonate with you? Have you recently or are you now experiencing "complete disorder and confusion"? Does your world appear "unpredictable" and "random"? Have you frequently observed that little things can unexpectedly throw you out of sorts and off track?

When this happens, your determined effort loses traction, and you may find yourself thinking, "What's the point, anyway?" That is how chaos can negatively affect you. But here is something else you need to know: chaos is also caused by an overabundance of seemingly positive conditions, such as explosive growth, rapidly increasing demand, and multiple promising paths of opportunity. And that's why I've called this book *Positive Chaos*. Let it be your key to unlocking the most powerful, beneficial aspects of our extraordinary times. The truth is:

- What you're experiencing isn't personal. It's universal.

- Chaos isn't necessarily negative. It's neutral.

- What seems "random" may not be. There are patterns at work you can see and shape to your benefit.

- You can harness the transformative power and energy of chaos to improve yourself, lead others, and accomplish more of what matters.

What if chaos could, in some or many ways, benefit you? After reading this book, not only will you know that waves of change are increasing in size and frequency, you will also understand why. You'll gain a basic understanding of chaos theory as I explore the origins, principles, and key discoveries of this fascinating, ever-expanding, multidisciplinary field of study. However, even though this may irk scientific or mathematical readers, I won't present specific equations or deep scientific research. My intention is to simplify the complex and help you apply universal concepts in life and business.

Positive Chaos will teach you both the *mindset* and the *skill set* for harnessing chaos to your advantage. You will learn specific ways to view your circumstances differently, as well as practical techniques to practice, hone, and share with others. As you progress in understanding, you'll see how these components overlap and serve each other. With the right mindset, your skills and actions will flow freely, and through practice and experimentation, you will gain a powerful personal perspective on the chaos in your life.

Seeing different perspectives has always been a strength of mine. This ability, or gift, instilled in me a natural curiosity and a desire to help others elevate their vision. I recognized this aspiration at an early age, which informed my education, entrepreneurial endeavors, and career track. After self-financing my business education by building an entertainment company, I shifted to the realm of corporate education and professional speaking. For nearly thirty years now, I've worked with leaders and workers on the front lines of business and professional development across a plethora of industries. Even though I have encountered vastly different circumstances on this journey, I've noticed people repeatedly face similar challenges.

These predictable challenges stem from the complexities of human nature and the difficulty of reconciling personal growth with change, external demands, and requirements for professional excellence.

I wrote the book *Off Balance On Purpose* because the dialogue on the subject of "achieving balance" was shallow and misinformed. That book has helped many thousands to see that "balance" is not what you get—an objective—it's what you *do* as you anticipate, adapt, and make adjustments. Similarly, *Positive Chaos* is an effort to set the record straight on chaos and provide new information, perspectives, and strategies for turning crisis and monumental change into opportunity and advantage.

Anchoring the ideas and insights throughout this book are illuminating and sometimes surprising findings from the first-of-its-kind research study that I mentioned earlier. The 2022 national study *Impact of Chaos in the American Workforce* was conducted in partnership with the Center for Generational Kinetics, a renowned research firm that specializes in behavioral research, or the human experiences and beliefs that lead to how people make choices and take action. The study's findings are statistically accurate within a margin of error of +/- 3.1 percent (considered the "gold standard" of such research), so you can be confident that the findings represent an accurate portrayal of how chaos is affecting people who are working full-time or part-time, are self-employed, or are actively looking for work throughout the United States and across various ages and demographics. Also, when I share these results with my international clients, they confirm that many of these same issues are impacting people worldwide.

The responses and insights that I'll share with you in this book from this study may resonate with you personally. But if you manage or lead a team, the findings will also be useful in areas of recruitment, performance, and employee satisfaction. The study also reveals opportunities for nurturing leadership development, increasing loyalty, and encouraging innovation. The following are some key findings of the study:

- Most working Americans are experiencing multiple aspects and detrimental effects of chaos in their personal and professional lives.

- Significant generational, gender, and job role or level of responsibility differences exist when it comes to personal and professional chaos perceptions, navigating chaos, leading through chaos, and transforming chaos into opportunity.

- People are motivated to transform and overcome the chaos in their lives through personal challenges and by working toward their goals.

Throughout this book, key statistics from the study will be inserted where they are most relevant to the text. To learn more about the study methodology and findings, and to download the white paper, visit **danthurmon.com/research.**

Beyond its business applications, this book will be valuable as you seek to reconcile the condition of chaos within your own life.

POSITIVE CHAOS is divided into three parts. The first part, simply called "Recognize," will help you understand how your current approach to accomplishment intersects with the condition of chaos. You'll learn the fundamental principles of chaos theory and how they apply to your life and business. This section will help you see the world differently and allow you to recognize those patterns at work in your life that serve you well and those that keep you mired in repeating loops of frustration.

Part Two is called "Respond," and it shows you how to upgrade your response system so you can dramatically change your results for the better. You'll learn how to seize real-time opportunities. I'll share five specific transformations that will enable you, regardless of your circumstances, to transform negative chaos into Positive Chaos.

In Part Three, "Realize," I will help you claim the tangible, powerful results of these transformations, your new mindset, and improved skill set. You will learn how to reinforce your armor to withstand hardships and quickly turn negative circumstances and even negative people into opportunities and allies. You'll establish new metrics to mark your progress and become a positive disruptor and an authentic leader in life and business, guiding others through today's uncertainties and the amplified chaos yet to come.

Before you can change or contribute in a significantly better way, first you must see things differently. With guidance and practice, you will unlock new abilities, heightening your understanding and awareness while defusing fear. You will become an astute observer of your world, and of yourself, not to judge what is but simply to recognize patterns and possibilities. Along this journey, you'll begin to see beyond illusions and distractions to glimpse both undeniable truth and unknowable mystery.

Let's get started by testing positive.

PART ONE
RECOGNIZE

The majority of working Americans would
immediately feel peace of mind if
they were able to develop their mindset
and skill set to better navigate chaos.

Impact of Chaos in the American Workforce,
danthurmon.com/research

1

Testing Positive

ITH MORE information at your fingertips than ever before, you might think living in an ordered universe would be easy, or at least achievable. But with twenty-four-hour news cycles, endless streams on social platforms, publications, books, and podcasts all growing exponentially, the cacophony of information and opinion is deafening. This noise makes it incredibly difficult for us to understand anything fully, much less keep up with the relentless pace and endless answers to the simple, innocent question, "Excuse me, can you please just tell me what's going on?"

If this is happening to you, then, without a doubt, you have tested positive for chaos.

Chaos is a condition. We experience it in our thinking and actions and when we observe events that impact us and people we know—family, friends, coworkers. When you are experiencing chaos, you attempt to reconcile your current reality and past experiences with what is happening in a "global" sense. But like any condition, chaos is subjective, based upon our individual experience. My chaos isn't your chaos. In fact, hearing about your chaos may freak me out even more, further complicating my chaos!

As you read this book, now is the time to pay attention to how the word *chaos* is used far more frequently than ever in the news and in private conversations. When you hear that word, ask yourself, "What is the intention?" Are the voices who proclaim chaos seeking to empower you or instill fear? Do you feel curious and informed or confused and afraid?

A Crisis of Chaos

We are living in an era where both the word *chaos* and its condition are amplified and intensified. This happens organically, as our systems become more open, complex, and global. These systems include politics, health care, financial policy, environment, culture, and countless other rapidly changing systems. Why is this happening?

Part of the amplification is, I believe, extremely intentional. In a world where leaders, companies, and governments seek to consolidate power and shape the future, chaos is a tool used to manipulate masses and accelerate change. This isn't conspiracy theory. It's part of the playbook. The concept of a "useful crisis" comes to mind. It benefits some to keep you unsettled, disrupted, and afraid. A frightened you is easier to manage and manipulate. The world doesn't advocate for your mental health and well-being. Some outside forces would rather you be reactive, afraid, small, angry, resentful, obsessed, and compliant: Don't think for yourself or discover your greatness—the world wants you weak, broke, and out of shape. Eat this. Buy that. Finance everything. Not because they hate you, but because "little you" helps some become bigger and more powerful.

Regardless of whether this is a result of circumstance or intention, the concept of "dealing with change" is the omnipresent experience of *chaos*. And for many people, that condition takes the following form:

CHAOS: Challenging, Hectic, Anxious, Overwhelming Stress

Challenging: you feel bombarded with difficulty and complex problems.

Hectic: the speed of change makes you feel behind constantly.

Anxious: you experience uncertainty as nervousness, dis-ease, and worry.

Overwhelming: the burden seems too great, and it's all on you to manage.

Stress: you feel unbearable pressure and unceasing tension.

This concept of chaos is increasing and is not producing happy, adjusted, highly functioning human beings. According to our *Impact of Chaos* study, it's quite the opposite. I invite you to sit with these unsettling findings for a moment:

- 79 percent of participants think not being able to handle chaos well leads to mental health challenges.

- 76 percent of participants believe chaos shortens people's lives.

- 62 percent of working Americans say that chaos has taken an emotional toll on them and their families in ways they didn't expect.

Also, specifically because of perceived chaos, participants indicated they experience these unsettling thoughts *at least once, daily*:

- 48 percent feel concern for family members.

- 43 percent feel anxiety.

- 37 percent feel overwhelmed.

- 24 percent consider giving up.

- 6 percent consider suicide.

This means if you have a hundred employees within your company, twenty-four of them are considering quitting and six of them think about suicide *every day* because they don't have the tools or ability to adequately cope with the chaos of their lives.

Without a doubt, there is a crisis of chaos in the experience of those working full-time, part-time, are self-employed, or are actively seeking employment. Although there are variations among generations, roles, and genders (I will explore that more later), the impact of today's experience of chaos is profound and disturbing.

Now that I have your attention, let me tell you the good news. This version of chaos and mindset of perpetual struggle is not the only way to view your world. It has been forced upon you and willingly accepted, much like a skilled magician offering you a "free choice" from a deck of cards.

But chaos is neither inherently good nor bad. It's neutral, and certainly not novel. In every era in human history, people have encountered massive disruptions, uncertainty, seemingly random hardships, fear and injustice, tragedy, dreams, desires, triumphs, and disappointments. The specifics have changed, and the present always seems more urgent and intense, but is it really all that different? Yes and no.

"Do you truly know what is positive and what is negative? Do you have the total picture? There have been many people for whom limitation, failure, loss, illness, or pain in whatever form turned out to be their greatest teacher. It taught them to let go of false self-images and superficial ego-dictated goals and desires. It gave them depth, humility, and compassion. It made them more real."

Eckhart Tolle, *The Power of Now*

You will soon understand the polarity of chaos you experience daily—chaos can be negative or positive. Instead of Challenging, Hectic, Anxious, Overwhelming Stress, you can see it as

Challenging: you select or accept difficult tests, seeing them as necessary *and* worthwhile.

Healthy: you contribute sustainable effort by prioritizing mental and physical wellness.

Aspiring: you orient yourself regularly to a positive future outlook.

Ongoing: you improve dysfunctional patterns by establishing better precedents.

Synergy: you see the connectedness and multiplied benefits in life's complexities.

The trick is to intentionally and consistently choose a perspective that serves you. One that will transform your experience of living while helping you achieve success and influence.

The Eternal Battle Between Chaos and Order

Humans have forever tried to make sense of reality and find purpose in the uncertainty of life. This quest has taken the form of a battle between what could be understood, organized, managed, and controlled versus what is unknown and uncontrollable. Order or chaos. In this archetype, chaos is evil, and order is good. Each new discovery and achievement brings us closer to good, and every threat to harmony or understanding brings us one step closer to doom.

The American comedy television show *Get Smart* (1965-70), created by Mel Brooks and Buck Henry, took this concept a step further. Maxwell Smart, played by Don Adams, was Agent 86, working for CONTROL (the good guys) along with his partner Agent 99 (played by Barbara Feldon) to uncover sinister plots and thwart the arch-enemy organization known as KAOS. In 2008 this concept was replayed in a major motion picture starting Steve Carell and Anne Hathaway.

You can see the parallels in countless works of fiction and portrayals of reality, dating back to the earliest days of recorded history. Chaos versus order is also a present-day theme of leadership. End the chaos, reclaim control, and return us to order. Do whatever it takes to stop the madness and bring back sanity and simplicity. Please be our hero. Save the day!

The problem is that, as with any archetypal idea like this, just because you can envision it doesn't mean it's possible or even beneficial. As you'll learn in future chapters, chaos and order aren't polar opposites. They coexist. They are interrelated and connected, two sides of the same coin. There may be order in what you currently perceive as chaotic, and amid the unknowable and seemingly random circumstances, there exist predictable opportunities.

Although order can provide discipline and functionality, it can also constrict options and opportunities. Order may be liberating or limiting. Likewise, chaos can be crushing or cathartic. What you currently perceive as chaos exists *within* order that you simply don't yet understand. There exists a power that you can use, regardless of your lack of understanding. Even within chaotic circumstances where you have little or no certainty, you can learn to achieve powerful clarity and take confident action by orienting to intention and principles.

As long as there is humanity (and, frankly, even if there isn't), there will be chaos. It serves us as much or more than it threatens but only *if* we can understand its power and true nature. I will help you attain that understanding and give you the ability to leverage the power of chaos to your advantage. But the chaos of the past isn't the chaos of today, and we need to understand how it's different to gain that leverage.

Are You in Data Overload?

Today's chaos is faster paced and highly amplified by technology, media, and our collective addiction to content. It's not enough for us to experience our world, think, comprehend, and act. We are growing accustomed to being told what to think and how to act. In a real sense, many people aren't interpreting their circumstances and responding thoughtfully. We're being programmed.

Every day, a massive amount of new information, text, audio, and video is added to the Internet, instantly searchable and broadcast to every connected corner of the world. The sheer volume of content drives the pace, implying that you might be able to "keep up" if you just make more of an effort. The priority is what's new right now, and rarely is yesterday's content (or last week's) scrutinized or analyzed. If you missed it, you missed it. If it wasn't accurate, it doesn't matter anymore. Move on. What's new now?

Again, this phenomenon isn't inherently good or bad, evil, or altruistic. It simply is. Yes, some of the information is manipulative or driven by fear. However, a great amount of new content is also generated by people with a desire to help others and provide encouragement, education, entertainment, or insights. The intentions and motives of content creators take countless forms and applications, but it is imperative that every consumer take responsibility and apply scrutiny to what they consume.

That can be especially difficult when the algorithms of social media platforms and news syndicators give you more of what you already know and believe. This has the effect of feeding confirmation bias, dividing groups, and driving behavior—what you buy, how you vote, and what you think about others. Thankfully, more and more, people are learning to discern what is and isn't beneficial, what's well intended and what's manipulative, and what is truly helpful and what may be harmful. It is exciting for me to watch those who are harnessing the chaos of our times to create connection and shortcuts to their aspiring visions.

Shortcuts

For generations, many of us have told our kids some version of this notion: "There are no shortcuts in life. Work hard. Pay your dues. Be patient. And your day will come." This is a noble idea that teaches important values and life skills such as discipline, humility, hard work, and delayed gratification. Today, however, this notion is not entirely true, or at least not the only path.

No longer do artists need agents to reach audiences. They have not one, but many platforms to go direct to the world. For those interested in a career, or skill, or field of study, the answers aren't behind the walls and tuitions of exclusive universities. Those answers are on your screens and at your fingertips if you simply search and have the attention and willingness to learn. Want to connect to people you respect and admire, or network your way to an opportunity? What's stopping you? The paths to would-be mentors and role models are limited only by your imagination.

Clearly there are shortcuts now. Lots of them.

Take, for example, Maggie, who was a high school senior when the pandemic hit. She had studied acting and music from a young age, was involved in summer acting camps, and learned how to play a little piano and guitar and write her own music. She was involved in high school theater and dabbled in film acting by being cast in a couple small parts in local movies. She is a natural comic, cracking up her parents even before she could talk. Maggie also knew something about social media, having worked as a "brand ambassador" for the clothing company Hollister during high school.

When the social media platform TikTok arrived, Maggie decided to dive in. She experimented with content until she discovered what clicked with her followers. Her platform went viral, and her following grew to not just thousands, but millions. She was contacted by a Los Angeles agent, who saw huge potential, especially considering her family-friendly content was a great fit for various brands. Within a year, Maggie was earning six figures in branding deals and exploring her real ambition, film acting. By the age of nineteen, she had moved to Los Angeles and expanded her online audience to over 5 million. She developed friendships with other influencers and content creators she long admired. She landed one of her first film auditions and a feature role in a major motion picture. And she's just getting started.

Maggie's story is one of many examples of individuals recognizing opportunity amid the chaos and taking charge of circumstances to create an untraditional shortcut to success. Watching Maggie's success unfold has been incredible, especially because I'm her dad (more on that story as the book unfolds). The key concept here is that when traditional paths are altered, new opportunities often emerge. As negativity and anxiety "scale up," so does the potential for positive impact, but *only if you know what you desire and how to engage with the chaos.*

Side note: If you currently believe TikTok is corrupting the world, programming our youth, and sending all our personal information to China, well, you may be right. There are certainly negative aspects to the platform, including its addictive nature, some of the content it showcases, and the company's aggressive data capturing. If that's all you focus on, it can seem scary and bleak. But if you also recognize TikTok's educational role and how it elevates amazing thinkers, teachers, and artists to new, worldwide audiences, then TikTok has proved pretty darn positive. Everything in life has pros and cons. To argue one exists without the other is to miss the full picture.

But negativity can be fun, and sometimes necessary. Right?

Sure, we are drawn to the negative, in part, to explore our polarity and more salacious desires: give me the scoop, the inside gossip. We want the *real* story about those people, or that issue, or our own darker nature. Part of this tendency is fueled by our own preservation instinct. Also, tragic stories are riveting! And it feels good and righteous to be actively opposed to someone or something because you genuinely despise it or them. But what is the effect of that kind of negativity?

My dad had a lot of wise and memorable sayings, which could also be quite amusing. One of my favorites is, "Never mud wrestle with a pig. You both get dirty, and the pig likes it." The relevant point is that when you get drawn into controversy and battle negativity with negativity, you depart from your true nature and only create a bigger mess.

In many ways it can be easier to stand against something, than to stand for what you love, value, and believe. You may feel you are being righteous without drawing too much attention to yourself. You're highlighting what you hate or find intolerable and wrong without being personally accountable. Never mind your own life, and your own shortcomings. You're only human. But you're a high-minded human who understands wrong when you see it!

Standing *for* something, however, requires you to plant a flag in the ground and say: This is what matters to me. I see value and beauty in the world. Also, once you plant your flag, you bring attention to how you live. Are you expressing the principles you champion? Or are you a hollow suit? A walking, talking contradiction? Later in the book (Chapter 13), I will lead you through a process to discern specific, powerful principles and values you will stand for. But for now, in terms of polarity, it's time to get positive.

Seeing the Positive

There is a more beneficial approach to engaging with today's increased uncertainty and chaos. It starts with *positive recognition*—seeing the world differently and noticing opportunities in real time. Implicit in this ability is the belief that there is not one way to see your world, but many. You can focus on the fear and negativity, doubt the motivations of everyone you meet, and see all of your circumstances working against you. Or, you can intentionally choose more positive beliefs, perspectives, and opinions. Presume that the people in your life are not motivated by wicked intentions, but by good nature. Recognize that their shortcomings are driven by limited perceptions and fear-based views. As you increase your ability to flip the polarity of a challenge into an opportunity, or at least defuse your attachment to your default negativity to a more neutral state, take notice of how it changes your options and influence.

As you read and implement the positivity tests in the skillset exercise for this chapter, measure your feelings about it. Does it seem silly and pointless? Give it a try anyway. Are some of these difficult for you? Do you notice a difference in how you feel or what happens as a result? Here you are beginning to test your ability to wield Positive Chaos in small ways. And, as you'll soon learn, that's often all it takes to make an enormous difference.

Of this, we can be positively certain: You get one life. There are no do-overs. Emboldened by the chaos and challenges you face, will you choose to seize this lifetime as an irrevocable opportunity to transform yourself, accomplish meaningful pursuits, and positively influence others? Or will you succumb to the distractions and challenges and lower your standards and expectations? I choose the former, and I sincerely hope you'll join me.

Turn the page to learn how to get more of what you want.

SKILLSET EXERCISE
POSITIVE TESTERS

Try these ten practical ideas to test your current comfort level with positivity and what happens when you choose positive over negative or neutral.

1 **Positive bookends.** Begin and end your day by reading, viewing, or saying something positive. Whatever happens in between, resolve to make the first and last intentional input each day something that makes you feel better. This could be a photo of a loved one, reading something inspiring, reviewing your goals and intentions, or speaking loving words to your partner. Mix it up. Stack your days and nights with positive bookends.

2 **Suspend your judgment.** Before you label something as good or bad, see that it just "is." Resist the impulse to assign a quality or character to your circumstances.

3 **Flip the script.** What if something you're calling a problem is actually part of the solution? Ask yourself, "What's the upside or opportunity?"

4 **Shift to serve.** Rather than being right or getting what you want, try to be helpful.

5   **Use names.** Whenever possible, use the names of the people you interact with. Try this even with your server or checkout cashier (by reading their nametag) and notice the jolt of positivity in them when they hear their own name.

6   **Offer a compliment.** When you notice something that impresses you about someone, say so.

7   **Provide encouragement.** When you notice or sense someone is struggling, find a way to encourage them.

8   **Do a secret good deed.** Do something for someone without being asked, without getting noticed, and without telling anyone what you did.

9   **Do just for you.** Do a kindness for yourself; treat yourself with greater care, love, and importance. Express some self-love.

10   **Smile.** Change your resting face to a smiling face and notice a shift in how you feel. Share a smile with a stranger and feel the energy exchange.

2

How to Get
What You Want

PRIOR TO the pandemic I was traveling on airplanes nearly every week to deliver keynote presentations at live events. In early March of 2020, I attended three conferences back-to-back. I spoke for Microsoft in Israel, then flew to Nashville for another client, then to Dallas for a third event located at the Gaylord Texan Resort & Convention Center. The Gaylord Texan is normally a bustling event facility with ten-thousand-plus guests and at least a dozen simultaneous meetings. But on March 10, 2020, there was exactly one meeting—the one at which I was engaged to speak. There were 150 people in the entire complex, and we all knew, beyond any doubt, the world had changed.

Within a few days after returning home, all my in-person events were cancelled, or at least postponed for the foreseeable future. Yet people and companies needed help more than ever, and especially in my areas of expertise: leading people through uncertainty, helping with work-life alignment, resilience, and reinvention.

Like so many others, my team and I had to pivot quickly. We transformed our existing video production studio into a robust digital broadcasting facility, equipped with five cameras, three different sets (for various functions), computers, video integration, interactive screens, and the capability to conduct live events with audiences of all sizes, anywhere in the world. This was an incredibly (and somewhat surprisingly) exciting time for the team and also stimulated our proactive, mission-driven purpose. We decided to get busy even though the world was in shock.

Instead of looking at this change in how we delivered our content as a temporary fix or a "less than" substitute, we saw the uncertainty and disruption as an enormous opportunity to stretch our skills and abilities beyond their previous scope and impact. Our response to the chaos was to elevate our brand, lead our industry, and authentically embody what we believe and teach to clients: *if you limit yourself to what's comfortable, you deny yourself what's possible.*

Our story is not unique. In many cases, businesses and individuals used this period of "forced disruption" to innovate, learn, and implement new initiatives in record time. But simultaneously, many businesses failed. Relationships ended. Academic pursuits had to be adjusted or stalled out entirely. And sadly, instances of depression and anxiety skyrocketed across all demographics. So, here's my question:

What enabled some people and companies to successfully pivot, thrive, and adjust to new circumstances, while others floundered helplessly?

I recognize this question could be perceived as insensitive and naïve. Clearly some people faced hardships, loss, illness, and disruption in far greater, more debilitating ways than others. I certainly don't want to diminish the suffering and challenges of our world. Instead, I'd like to understand how to *transcend them* more effectively. Perhaps the larger questions, ones I have pondered throughout three decades of helping people and organizations, leaders and professionals, dreamers and artists, inventors and entrepreneurs, are these:

- Why do some persevere, and others give up?

- Why do some grow and learn, and others flounder?

- And why do some succeed, while success eludes other people repeatedly?

During more than thirty years in this business, as I have consulted with hundreds of leaders in a vast array of industries, met with high performance teams, and delivered thousands of presentations all around the world, I've found a way to answer these complex questions with the WAC Model. This model will help you discover the limitations you face personally or discern why the teams or organizations you belong to may be struggling.

The WAC Model

For ease of understanding, I'll present this model as a Venn diagram, with three overlapping circles. The first of these circles is willingness.

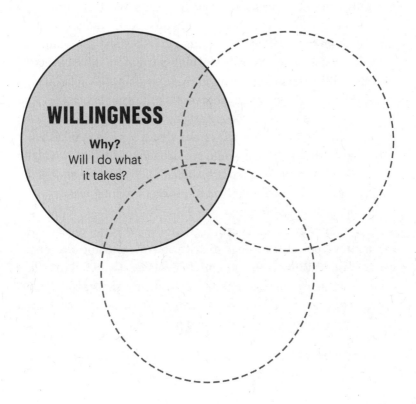

Willingness

W stands for willingness: not "wanting" or "working" but being truly *willing* to do what it takes—whatever it takes—to accomplish a goal, strengthen a relationship, change a behavior, or achieve any other desirable ambition. Willingness is the answer to the question, "Why does this matter?" Desire alone is insufficient. You must take action and exert your will.

The answer to this question, "Why does this matter?," must be persuasive enough to overcome inertia, struggles, challenges, and the possibility of failure. But here's the truth. For most people, that answer simply isn't sufficiently compelling.

People may profess their willingness, express desire, or even make the case for change. But when pressed to address their level of commitment, they buckle or hedge. Someone may be willing to go with the program or pursue a course of action temporarily. But when faced with immense difficulty and complex problems, they pull back from the commitment instead of leaning in to embrace the challenge.

True willingness is predicated on ownership. Not just owning your job or your responsibility, but owning the entire outcome. And here's the problem: When you are asked, "Are you willing to do what it takes?" you often don't really know what it's going to take! What you thought the challenge would require of you yesterday may be revealed today to be completely insufficient. At that moment of discovery, are you still willing? The question of willingness must be asked and answered every day.

Is your answer to the question about the potential upside (why this matters) powerful enough to drive you to overcome challenges yet unknown? What is the potential downside if you fail to follow through? In sports contests among great athletes, victory isn't always attained by the most talented competitor, but by the person or team who wanted it more. Those who had more will to win, or, perhaps, who were unwilling to lose.

Increase Willingness

But how do you increase willingness? The following approaches can be effective.

Amplify the upside

One answer to the questions "Why does this matter?" and "Am I willing to do what it takes?" resides in the form of flat-out compensation: I will pay you to care. If I want you to care more, I can pay you more or offer something else of value in exchange for your "all-in" effort. Although this approach has limitations, it's often practiced in the workforce and throughout human interactions.

Some parents compensate their children when they do their chores or make good grades. Have you ever asked friends to help you move and offered to buy pizza and beer afterward? Although the situation isn't exactly an equal exchange, when you ask for something it's always useful to have an "upside" to offer in return. Reciprocity is part of our culture and makeup. You want me to do what? What's in it for me?

For most people, receiving recognition and positive feedback and participating in fulfilling relationships are powerful "upsides," and they are also useful in motivating action.

Clarify the downside

The classic metaphor of the carrot and the stick captures the idea behind asking which is more effective in creating willingness and motivation: rewards (positive upside) or punishments (potential negative consequence)? The answer is, it depends. The human brain's limbic system generally responds favorably to reward when it comes to reinforcement. When you want to encourage or promote more of a behavior, upsides are effective. If, however, you seek to discourage a specific behavior, it is generally agreed among behavioral researchers that the promise of negative consequences seems to work better. Pain is more powerful than pleasure when getting us to stop doing something. This is definitely the case when it comes to personal improvement.

Behavior modification is difficult for most people. Seeing the upside of making changes to your behavior can be useful motivation, but avoiding pain, death, and destruction usually wins the day. Many alcoholics and addicts only seek help once they've reached rock bottom. Smokers quit more easily after receiving a frightening diagnosis or seeing X-rays of damaged lungs. The same can be true for other behavior changes, including weight loss and relationship patterns. Once you realize what's at risk, willingness generally increases.

How does this serve us in the workplace? A zero-tolerance policy on safety violations or inappropriate behavior can certainly be an effective deterrent, provided the regulations are communicated, understood, and enforced.

Power up your purpose

Humans are incredibly compelled by purpose. We want our jobs and lives to have meaning. We want to know and follow great leaders. We want to be a part of a mission or cause that genuinely *matters* in the world, so that we can look back and know we made a meaningful difference. What's interesting is that perceived chaos can intensify this motivation. When life seems random, chaotic, and uncontrollable, it becomes easier to distinguish what matters. And although you may be facing considerable challenges, you become more *willing* when engaged with something necessary, important, and personal.

Extend your empathy

Humans have a deep need to be understood. We are more willing to follow a leader or team who knows and values others' perspectives and circumstances. This became clear during the COVID pandemic, when many employees experienced professional disruption and personal hardships simultaneously. Some leaders and organizations immediately saw the opportunity to demonstrate how much they valued their people and doubled down on their intention to support them.

This took the form of accommodating needs, providing education and technology, and finding new ways to get work done. We collaborated with many great leaders who understood what was at stake for their people and saw this period as an opportunity to elevate their culture and mission. This approach went a long way to increase willingness of their team to do "what it takes," even when things were extremely uncertain. Going forward, these same organizations are attuned to the reality that the workplace is forever changed. They are seeking to find new agreements and approaches to work that continue to support and serve their people. I'll introduce you to some of these leaders, strategies, and agreements in Chapter 16.

Unfortunately, we also saw the opposite scenario unfold. Some leaders and organizations did not empathize with their teams. Driven by fear and scarcity, they failed to grasp the enormity of the challenges people were experiencing personally. Instead of taking the approach of "this is hard, we understand what you're experiencing, and we'll get through these days together," they sent mixed signals: "We get this is difficult but still need you to do whatever is necessary for as long as it takes." Lacking empathy, some leaders destroyed willingness at the time when it was most needed. Many people lost jobs, quit, or, perhaps even worse, kept their positions but lost their willingness and desire.

When people aren't willing, but remain working, they may seem productive, engaged, and committed. However, they may just be going through the motions.

Building a Boat

I was nine in the summer of 1977 when my friends and I gathered in my tiny back yard (twenty-eight feet wide) to plan our adventure. We would gather materials, tools, and supplies, and construct a boat. Before the end of the summer and the start of school, we planned to launch our vessel into Lake Michigan and sail the open waters. This goal had it all! Teamwork, creativity, and, ultimately, a heroic, epic voyage. It was exciting, and probably an early test of my leadership.

Friends quickly started hauling over wood from their homes or salvaged from local trash sites. Others joined the cause. We sawed, hammered, and screwed things together with our parents' tools and, little by little, watched our creation take shape. It was quickly evident that our boat would not float. It was too heavy and definitely not waterproof. So, we had our mothers save milk jugs. The plan was to seal the jugs and attach them to the underside of the deck, providing extra buoyancy.

All through the summer, day after day, we worked, sweat, (at times) bled, laughed, and sang. We shared stories of our future adventure as we watched our boat take form. Finally, at the end of the summer, our project reached its inevitable conclusion: everyone went home, we never sailed the boat, and no one was surprised. The reason is clear in retrospect. We were building a boat, busily working, and sharing a collective imagination. But we all knew on some level we were never really going to launch it.

We weren't truly *willing* to follow through on that intention. If we had been, we would have gone about this project differently, with a lot more attention to detail. We would have consulted with experts, conducted tests, and definitely done a lot more research. When it came down to it, we were just spectacularly pretending.

How many people right now can claim to be in pursuit of their dreams, but are just "building a boat"? How many teams and organizations are busily engaged with a project or task but without any true attachment to the outcome? They may be wanting. They may be working. But they're not *willing*.

Willingness requires that you are honest with yourself. If you are unwilling to get real with yourself and those around you, what are you really doing? Spectacularly pretending. Willingness, true willingness, is an absolute prerequisite for accomplishment, growth, and success. But it's not without limitations.

The Limitations of Willingness

Here are three common areas where willingness falls short. Whether you are leading a team or monitoring your own progress, stay alert to notice when these factors enter the equation.

You can't outsource willingness

You can't make someone "want it" as much as you, or more than you. I often encounter leaders and entrepreneurs who complain about their teams. "They're just not motivated and driven enough to achieve my goals, objectives, and dreams." And there's the problem: it's your dream, and apparently not theirs. You can't outsource willingness; it starts with you, and then must also be cultivated in those you depend on.

Willingness is dynamic

Willingness within an individual or organization requires feeding, care, rest, and renewal. It will ebb and flow depending on the challenges, threats, and demands of the immediate moment. For that reason, effective leaders and driven individuals consistently check the pulse of willingness within themselves and those around them. When willingness begins to wane or falter, this is an opportunity for you to revisit your personal or organizational purpose, to clarify your goals and strategy, to provide encouragement to your team, or facilitate rest and recovery.

Willingness alone is not enough

Being willing doesn't overcome all obstacles. Just because you want it doesn't mean it's possible. Willingness won't nullify a bad business plan, subpar offering, or basic lack of competence. It can, however, create the necessary motivation to adapt your plan, improve your offering, and move mere competence to excellence.

WILLINGNESS IS the most critical prerequisite to accomplishment. It is the foundation of all that matters, and the chief determinant of whether you will persevere and succeed or lose steam and fail. For that reason, I've devoted the bulk of the discussion in this chapter to this first sphere. In future chapters, we will continue to address this model and the remaining components in greater depth, but for now, let's introduce the second component of accomplishment: ability.

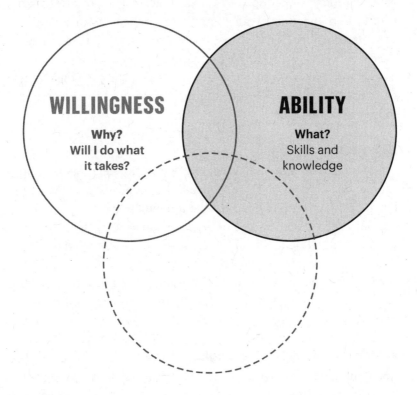

Ability

Ability is the answer to the question, "What does it take?" Once you have found your willingness, you can accomplish what's necessary, and that means developing your skills and expanding your knowledge. Think about how you would answer the following questions:

- What must you know and become capable of doing?

- What is the existing gap between what you desire and your ability to execute?

- What skills and capabilities must you or your team develop?

- In what areas will you move beyond competence to become a true expert?

As with willingness, you can see that these questions apply to individuals and organizations. Effective people see themselves as capable learners with ever-expanding skill sets. Great organizations develop a culture of learning and ever-increasing abilities. They accomplish this by providing access to training and development, formal and informal mentoring, and a shared curiosity and awareness that there will always be more to learn. How about you?

- Do you have an appetite to learn new ideas and skills?

- Are you genuinely curious about your world?

- Do you have both professional ambitions and personal pursuits that drive and excite you?

- Do you devote time and energy to practicing skills and learning new information, apart from your active projects and current workload?

When the pandemic hit, much of what we previously thought important became irrelevant, at least for the short term. What that revealed in the process was how astute and attuned you were to what was required, and how willingly or eagerly you were able to adapt. How did you do? Did you "lean in" eagerly to learn new skills? Did you seek guidance from others further along in the journey than you?

Improvement is a choice before it becomes a process or a result. Learning takes time and dedicated practice. Be realistic in assessing your current ability and identifying the gaps. What exactly are you trying to *improve*? Why does this matter? Who do you seek to emulate and learn from? How will you measure progress? When will you know you've made a breakthrough or significant stride forward?

Ability isn't hypothetical. Either you can, or you cannot. Your professional value is directly tied to your ability to recognize and provide what is needed, useful, and effective. In a chaotic world, this requires expansive understanding and adaptive problem-solving. Making it work. Jumping into uncertainty saying, "let's figure this out as we go." Can you convert your knowledge into action and results when the pressure is on? As you progress through this book, you will learn how to identify and advance critical skills more effectively.

For now, the brutal truth is that many people who start this book won't finish it (not you). Many people who say they are willing, and genuinely feel so, will lose their way. And even if you sustain your willingness, and map the course to developing abilities, skills, and knowledge, you may not get there. Unfortunately, many people give up or fall short of what they intend. They lose willingness and settle for less. Their curiosity diminishes, and they don't develop their abilities. In my view, that's because they fail to adequately understand and address the third component of the WAC Model.

Capacity

If willingness is the answer to the question "why?" and ability is the answer to the question "what?," then capacity is the answer to the question "how much?" How much can you handle? How much can you absorb? What is your bandwidth for life?

You see, it's easy to envision endless accomplishments when thinking about what we want to achieve and making lists. We make commitments and accept obligations. That's important and, to a degree, necessary to become a capable, respected, highly functioning person. But your capacity, like willingness, is not limitless. You have only so much time, thought, energy, money, and other resources. How will you allot what you have to become what you envision and accomplish what you desire?

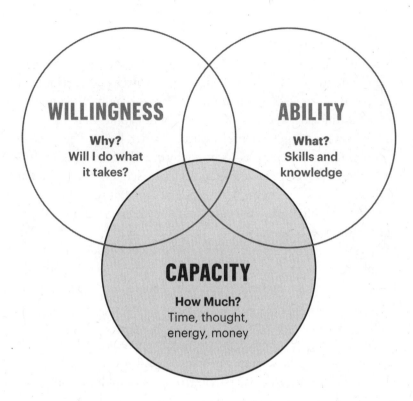

The good news is that even though your capacity is finite, it isn't fixed. You can expand your capacity. You can warp time to learn faster and make a profound impact more quickly. You can expand your thinking to higher levels of effectiveness and power. You can increase and better manage your energy. And you can expand resources while using them more effectively.

I've proved this concept hundreds of times on stages in front of live audiences with an unsuspecting volunteer. I set up a scenario in which I teach the participant (whom I've never met before) to learn a new skill they've never attempted in a matter of just a few minutes. I teach them to "half juggle" with me, each of us throwing balls into the air, side by side, across to one another, to create and sustain a three-ball juggling pattern.

I help this person expand their capacity by first addressing beliefs. Specifically, asking "Do you think this is possible?" In many cases, they start with serious doubts. Then I ask, "What if I support you and do half the work? Also, we will build upon your existing strengths, and you can use your dominant hand." By stretching their beliefs from the limiting doubt to open possibilities and helping them through a refined process, they invariably learn faster. The process becomes fun and exciting as I continually coach them through subsequent steps. We improve throws and catches, sequencing additional balls to the pulse of energetic music. The "breakthrough moment" is always a highlight, and the participant becomes a hero in the eyes of the audience. It never fails, and many of these people later tell me that this experience—proving they had greater capacity—enabled them to step more boldly into new challenges. This is exactly my aim with this book: to help shape your beliefs, to work with your strengths, and to teach and encourage you toward greater capacity, results, and future celebrations.

Time, thought, money, and energy are precious units of your capacity. Each can be squandered or invested. They could be devoted to one specific purpose, or expanded to advance multiple aspects of your desires, simultaneously. When aligned together, and toward a purposeful objective, the most amazing thing happens: *capacity expands*. This is why some people can simply accomplish more than others or are more comfortable in the unfolding of circumstances. They know that while they may not yet have sufficient skills, time, ideas, or dollars, they will have them at the moment required if they simply proceed forward with clear intention. They become creators of Positive Chaos. I'm getting ahead of myself, but I want you to know that this reality is truly possible and within your grasp as you implement the principles and strategies to come.

The other question that ties into capacity is: How comfortable are you amid change or even chaos? Are you easily thrown? Or can you remain grounded during a rapidly changing situation? What if you could raise the bar in this respect, expanding your capacity even slightly to access your creativity and confidence during chaos? Think of how that one small change might help you think more clearly, make more informed decisions, take better care of yourself, and be of greater value to others. Increasing your capacity even slightly could, over time, raise the contributions of your life to extraordinary levels.

In Part Two of this book, I will help you profoundly increase your capacity. Instead of seeing scarcity, you'll learn how to create synergy. You'll also gain the ability to discern, far more quickly, what is and what isn't worth your time, thought, and energy. This level of clarity will enable you to better navigate an intentional course, which you prescribe, as well as the chaos of uncertainty you cannot predict.

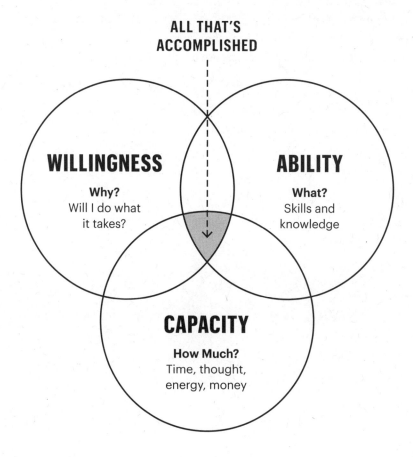

WHY AM I so passionate about willingness, ability, and capacity?

Think of it this way: all that ever gets accomplished, anywhere in the world by an individual or organization, exists in the overlap of those three aspects of the WAC Model. For a task to be accomplished or a dream to be realized, one must truly, deeply, honestly have the *willingness* to do what it takes, develop the *ability* to execute by acquiring knowledge and learning skills, and create the *capacity* within one's life or team to make it happen.

Also consider all those remarkable achievements happen during unique and challenging times of chaos. Success doesn't occur in a vacuum. It happens in concert with our messy, random, uncertain reality. So, what will you do when your ambitions inevitably encounter the forces of chaos?

Next, let's go deeper into what chaos truly is to find out how it can become your partner in creative and meaningful achievement.

SKILLSET EXERCISE
ASSESS YOUR WAC

Stop pretending and get real about your current state of willingness, ability, and capacity. You can apply this exercise to your work, relationships, or any personal undertaking. Answer these questions for yourself or with your team.

Willingness

1   What level of commitment do I bring to my job? What am I willing to do?

2   Can I increase my willingness by amplifying the upside, clarifying the downside, powering up purpose, or extending empathy?

3   What am I unwilling to do? (Note that by identifying and owning this, you're not admitting failure or defeat. You could be releasing unrealistic expectations.)

Ability

1   What skills, ability, and knowledge do I currently possess?

2   What abilities do I require that I don't presently have? What skills and knowledge will be needed in the future?

3   How will I bridge the ability gap?

Capacity

1   Considering my resources of time, energy, money, and thought, how close am I to operating at full capacity?

2   How can I create more capacity by releasing unnecessary obligations or distractions?

3   Am I prepared to relinquish some control or exactness in order to become more comfortable and capable in the midst of chaos?

3

Butterfly Effectiveness

WILLINGNESS, ABILITY, AND CAPACITY are critical to accomplishment. Yet we don't pursue our dreams in isolation, detached from the world or unaffected by others' goals and motivations. Here lies the essence of chaos: where your effort, expectations, and intentions meet uncertainty and randomness, creating complexity and unpredictable results.

In 1962, Edward Norton Lorenz was trying to predict the weather, and as both a mathematician and a climatologist, he was eminently qualified. After studying mathematics at Dartmouth College and Harvard University, Lorenz turned his attention and service with the Army Air Corps to weather forecasting in 1942. After World War II, he became a researcher at Massachusetts Institute of Technology, earning a master's degree, then a doctorate in meteorology.

As Lorenz attempted to construct models that could accurately determine future weather patterns, he discovered an impossible problem. No matter how much data he gathered, or how he constructed the models, he noticed parallel models would quickly diverge to very different, unpredictable paths. Quite frequently, two similar starting points would take completely divergent trajectories, resulting in remarkably different weather patterns: one calm, and another stormy.

Lorenz concluded that tiny, often imperceptible "inputs," or changes to the conditions, would produce huge differences across models and actual weather events. This served as the underlying mechanism of what became known as deterministic chaos, or chaos theory. Lorenz also coined the catchy term *butterfly effect* to describe how small air movements created by a butterfly flapping its wings in one part of the world could, theoretically, create or contribute to a weather system, potentially even resulting in a hurricane, hundreds of miles away.

Curiously, ten years before Lorenz's epiphany, in 1952, writer Ray Bradbury produced a science fiction short story entitled "A Sound of Thunder," set in the year 2055. In this future reality, time travel is not only possible, but commercialized, enabling high-rolling adventurers, in this case Eckels, to pay $10,000 to travel 65 million years into the past to hunt the ultimate predator, Tyrannosaurus rex. Technology enables time-traveling hunters to walk on an elevated path so they will not disturb the environment. Furthermore, their prey are carefully selected creatures who would have died anyway, precisely at the time of the hunt.

The hunting party is successful, killing the T-Rex at the precise moment before a tree fell that would have ended its life, regardless. But during the process Eckels lost his nerve and jumped off the path briefly. When Eckels and the hunting party return to 2055—spoiler alert—they find the world altered. Language is different, election outcomes have changed, and it quickly becomes obvious that something has disturbed the flow of time and events of history. Eckels looks at the bottom of his boot and sees a crushed butterfly, which implies that all these changes are the result of ripple effects, over the course of millennia, due to his mistake and the loss of one small life.

The term *butterfly effect* is sometimes attributed to Bradbury because of this story and its vivid example of deterministic chaos: one small, random input—involving a butterfly, no less!—creating hugely amplified, unknowable outputs. However, the term seems not to have come into use until Edward Norton Lorenz coined it ten years later. Was he influenced by Bradbury's story? Was this a clever nod to the author? An example of truth following fiction? It seems we will never know. For now, and when it comes to the persistence of the "butterfly," stay tuned, as that plot thickens. First let's talk a bit more about systems.

Systems and Complexity

Chaos and complexity exist within the physical or intellectual concept of a *system*. We live and operate within a multitude of systems. These include (as a small sampling) systems of government, law, finance, family, energy, transportation, commerce, thought, agriculture, power, and weather. Systems can be organic (such as a human body) or institutional (such as a student body). There exists a physical or psychological boundary separating that which is contained in the system (organic life, ideas, or things, for instance) from that which isn't contained in the system. The walls, real or imaginary, are constructed through shared agreements. A system exists because we have created it, constructed it, or concluded that it's real.

The more closed a system—meaning the more it is impervious to penetration or the passage of physical materials, energy, or ideas—the more stable and predictable it will be. *Isolated systems*, that allow nothing to transfer, are more theoretical in nature. *Closed systems* don't allow the passage of matter but do allow energy and information to exchange. *Open systems* have permeable boundaries that allow the passage of matter, energy, and information.

What is most important to understand here is that as openness and complexity increase within a system, so does potential chaos, the possibility or likelihood of uncertainty and randomness. And that is something you need to get comfortable with if you are going to work in the flow of Positive Chaos.

Today the free flow and interconnectedness of information worldwide means that the activities you are engaged in as an individual or business are conducted within larger, more open systems than ever before. This means your circumstances are fused with complexity, amplified by the speed of technology. Before you have an opportunity to fully process or respond to the complexity you encounter, it often changes, elevates, or intensifies.

For example, consumer brands used to manage customer engagement within an open system containing existing customers who purchased their products and services. They received direct feedback via customer service calls or email outreach. They may also have provided outreach to their customers to thank them for business, ask for feedback, offer new products and promotions, or solicit potential referrals. They sought to build a community of customers that was dynamic, yet manageable.

Today, however, in addition to previous forms of communication, brands engage with customers, non-customers, fans, and detractors on open social media platforms in front of a worldwide audience. To lodge a complaint or criticism, you don't even need to purchase the product. You can simply go online and visit the social media page of the company you wish to praise or admonish, or tag them from your own page, and do so publicly, in whatever language you choose. The post then takes on a life of its own, garnishing likes and comments in support.

Before the brand even sees the comment or has an opportunity to address it, the post often unfolds into a debate containing multiple opinions and erroneous information. Now, not only must the brand address the complaint, but it has to do so "on stage" in front of a frenzied audience. It's easy to see how this openness increases complexity and uncertainty. It also, however, creates new opportunity for brands to demonstrate authenticity and understanding.

Even our personal systems are far more open and complex than in previous eras. For instance, just one generation ago, the "family system" was remarkably different. When I was growing up, we had one phone in our kitchen, equipped with a twenty-foot-long spiraling cord, which could never quite stretch to a range of privacy. When you wanted answers, you asked your parents, visited the library, or consulted the *Encyclopedia Britannica* volumes in the living room. Seeing friends meant going over to someone's house or going out on an adventure. Either option involved getting permission. Within a family, it was easier to maintain structure, order, values, and plans. As for entertainment, we had games nights and one television, equipped with a few fuzzy channels. Consult the TV *Guide*, see what's on right now. Take it or leave it.

Contrast that to a generation later: not only does today's modern family have instant access to just about everything, but with the proliferation of smartphones, each family member (of a certain age) has their own limitless, unique, endless digital experience. Connecting with friends doesn't require permission or oversight. No longer do we need to share physical space at all. Need an answer? Forget mom and dad. Google it. Or watch a YouTube video. And as for entertainment, the choices are endless, with new content created in exponentially greater volume every day. Kids today aren't only consumers but also very likely *creators* of content, posting to Insta, Snap, TikTok, and likely other platforms we don't yet know about.

As first-generation parents of "tech kids," my wife and I have had to make decisions about access, usage, permissions, and devices in the fast-paced flow of life and a storm of opaque uncertainty. Is this good for them or harmful? Clearly the answer is, potentially both. How much is too much? We had to guess, in real time, about unknowable consequences, without any insight into what might be the long-term repercussions of our choices.

In retrospect, we might have been more prescriptive and restrictive. But these were uncharted waters, and, like all aspects of parenting, doing the "best thing" is exponentially more time-consuming and difficult than doing the "good thing." Our son, Eddie, was learning on a computer at the age of two. He and his sister were iPad masters. They both had smartphones by high school. They also both had instruments, activities, family time, shared meals, talk time, and nightly tuck-ins. We did our best to compensate for the undeniable chaos and complexity by fostering *stability* within our family system.

As we further examine the winds of change, let's return, as promised, to our weather-obsessed, mathematical friend, Edward Norton Lorenz.

Order Within Chaos

When Lorenz wanted to understand why he could not reconcile these small fluctuations in random weather phenomena, he started to plot the answers to randomly generated differential equations on a three-dimensional graph. Rather than producing scattered, disconnected data, what emerged in Lorenz's graph was a clear and distinctive pattern of infinite loops that repeated on various planes. Not only did this graph, named the Lorenz attractor, produce an orderly image of infinity sign loops, but it just happened to resemble the wings of a butterfly.

Lorenz's attractor

What does this mean exactly? Again, let me oversimplify to the chagrin of my scientifically astute readers.

Within a system, you look for attractors, or causative factors, to help understand what is happening or predict what might happen. Attractors are models that incorporate various forces that affect objects or elements in their processes and environments. Such forces could include, for example, gravity, temperature, pressure, wind, supply, demand, competition, or available resources. The environment, or phase space to use the scientific term, represents the playing field on which these operations take place. Lorenz's attractor, for example, represents great complexity and potential chaos, yet still reveals repeated patterns.

In physics and mathematics, there are four different types of attractors: fixed point, limit cycles, tori, and strange attractors. I'm going to define three of these, as they are most relevant to our discussion.

Fixed point attractors are the easiest to understand and quantify. They operate, as the name implies, with a single fixed point affecting an object. Imagine, for example, a weight hanging from a string. The fixed point of attraction, in this case, is gravity. Whether the weight is moved in a linear motion, as in a pendulum, or in circular motion, creating a spiral, or even in another more complex initial launch, it will exhibit predictable behavior and eventually come to rest at a fixed point.

Limit cycles do not come to rest (stillness) but operate within certain limits or parameters, like a heartbeat, for example. These also include "predator-prey" systems in some cases, whereby two or more factors influence and in certain ways "feed" off one another.

Strange attractors, or chaotic attractors, are unpredictable, dynamic, and, at times, bizarre. The Lorenz attractor is an example of a strange attractor. When dynamic forces are in play, you cannot predict from an initial starting point where you will end up. There is no consistent, predictable path. You can only conclude that you will end up somewhere within the model. (Tori attractors—in case you're wondering—exhibit qualities of limit cycles with some of the characteristics of strange attractors, resulting in their own unique, chaotic behavior. This idea is also relevant to our lives. But that's a "story" for another book!)

Strange attractors are why weather predictions, to this day, remain "best guesses within certain parameters." Yet it's also the environment in which we live, work, and pursue ambitions. Your understanding of what's happening is directly related to your cognitive model. If you view life from a single "fixed" focus, or as a "limit cycle" (it's either this or that, within these parameters), you're missing the majority of what's really happening. We live in a strange, chaotic system where everything affects everything, all the time.

Now, think about the attractors (dynamic forces) at work and play in your life. These could include your ideas, goals, beliefs, behaviors, ambitions, fears, obligations, or people in your life. Where do they come from, and how present and powerful are the forces they exert upon you? How do these attractors limit you? In what ways are they beneficial? How do they cause you to navigate repetitive loops of experience? Identifying and interrupting repeating, limiting loops and changing patterns for the better is the essence of Positive Chaos.

The combination of so many attractors pulling on your physical and mental reality is one of the most powerful and persistent reasons you experience the condition of chaos. But what if you could remove or weaken the force of the negative attractors in your life while strengthening more positive attractors? For instance, instead of spending time around people who discourage you, take advantage of you, or lower your self-esteem, what if you attracted accomplished people who inspire you? What if instead of clinging to limiting behaviors, old ideas, or broken tools, you could choose empowering ideas and better strategies? Little things change everything in very big ways.

What this all means is that making one small change could have the effect of altering your life immeasurably for the better.

Your Butterfly Effect

When you look back on your own life journey, can you identify moments or seemingly random encounters that literally shaped the course of your life? Perhaps you received encouragement from a friend, teacher, or parent. Perhaps you discovered a talent, were exposed to an idea, or were offered an opportunity that changed everything. One such moment happened for me at the King Richard's Renaissance Faire in Bristol, Wisconsin, in July 1979.

My mother, an artist, was persuaded by a friend and fellow artist, Jane Pitatsis, to build a booth at the King Richard's Faire (now called the Bristol Faire). For as long as I could remember, we had been going to art shows across Chicagoland, in parks, shopping malls, and all variety of locations to sell paintings and pet portraits. But we had never been to a show like this one. Sixteenth-century England was recreated with jousting knights, wild characters, masterful minstrels, amazing performers, and the court of a king and queen complete with their entourage. I was in heaven, dressed in my homemade costume, and blissfully lost in fantasyland.

After helping Mom get set up in her shop, I wandered around the festival and was captivated by a juggler named Mike Vondruska. He was amazingly talented at manipulation and performing. I watched his show all day, moving closer each performance until I was in the front row. He noticed. After the last show of the day, he called me over and said, "Hey kid, you've been here all day. Do you want to learn?"

That was it. Those five words changed everything. *Do you want to learn?* When you think of it, those five words are the essence of the question of *willingness*. Are you willing to invest attention, put in the practice, overcome frustration, claim incremental breakthroughs, and eventually arrive at a level of competence which you will then realize is only the beginning?

When I said yes to Mike at the King Richard's Faire at the age of eleven, my life was forever altered. Not only did I learn a skill, but I gained a true friend and mentor. In teaching me to juggle, Mike introduced me to the concept of learning patterns (quite literally, as juggling is about that very notion). He also introduced me to a larger community of performers.

This was a new and fascinating "system," and because of my interests and practice I *belonged*. I expanded my skill set to include unicycling, stilt walking, rope walking, and other unusual abilities. Mainly, however, I learned how to focus my mind and apply myself to challenging tasks. I learned to persist through difficulty to attain proficiency. Then, I learned how to take my talents to the stage, crafting a show and launching a performance career before I was a teenager.

Along this path, I also became fascinated about learning and excellence. How does mastery happen? Is it possible to shorten learning curves? These early questions started a lifelong course of study in personal development and self-mastery and led me to teachers and authors in the fields of motivation, neuro-linguistic programming, and peak performance. While I pursued my business degree at the University of Georgia, I grew my business from a one-man show into an entertainment production company, and, eventually, in my mid-twenties, into the world of professional speaking and corporate education.

As I think back upon my life journey, I wonder what was that first seemingly random input that created such a profound eventual output? Was it my mother's example? Mom's friend Jane inviting her to join the Faire? Was it Mike's simple question, "Do you want to learn?" Yes. All of the above and countless other "random inputs" contributed to Positive Chaos in my life. My hope is that you are beginning to understand and *believe* that you can harness this power and mathematical certainties to dramatically improve your own story.

Chaos Conclusions

Lorenz's butterfly effect offers two essential insights that are foundational to the concept of Positive Chaos.

1   **Random, seemingly imperceptible changes to inputs produce huge variations over time—amplified, unknowable future results.** Simply stated, little things change everything, in huge ways that cannot be fully comprehended. You get to choose how you will engage with this reality. You can fall victim to the unpredictable, feeling helpless and incapacitated, or you can use it to your advantage—that is the essence of the Positive Chaos mindset.

    And when you practice Positive Chaos, you consciously change your inputs—thoughts, words, and actions—sometimes in small but significant ways, while in the flow of your current chaos. As a result, you can trust with certainty that these changes will produce sizable future results. However, and here's the fun part, from any present moment, you cannot know exactly what those results will be.

2   **Underlying patterns will emerge.** What seems random and chaotic may not be. In fact, it almost certainly isn't. Even amid chaos and massive disruptions, underlying patterns exist. Look back at the image of Lorenz's attractor again. Within your own life, you've experienced countless patterns of repetitive loops—decisions and actions that perpetuate similar results and future decisions. As you own this understanding, you develop the ability to recognize the patterns of the past. You can respond differently in the present and by shaping the patterns in new ways, you will create new and amplified future results.

    As you think back on your life story, what are your examples of seemingly random inputs that resulted in big changes in your life? What are the inputs you encountered in your life that changed everything? Which of them created a course that you recognize as vital to your current existence? Which of those inputs created limiting or detrimental consequences? More importantly, what will you do now, having gleaned these insights?

You Can't Know Everything

Although Edward Norton Lorenz made significant contributions and put chaos theory squarely on the map, the origins and contributors to the field began long before he arrived on the scene. As humans began to understand the world, people desired to reconcile the observed and orderly with the unpredictable. The unpredictable was seen as the hand of God, or the mysteries of the universe beyond our understanding. Philosophy and science were inextricably linked.

Sir Isaac Newton (1642–1727) changed that construct in significant ways by contributing differential calculus and classical mechanics. This fueled the force of determinism—the notion that with straightforward analysis and mechanical mastery, we could understand our world *exactly*.

Pierre-Simon, marquis de Laplace (1749–1827) took determinism a step further, stating, "An intellect which at any given moment knew all of the forces that animate nature and the mutual positions of the beings that compose it, if this intellect were vast enough to submit the data to analysis, could condense into a single formula the movement of the greatest bodies of the universe and that of the lightest atom; for such an intellect nothing could be uncertain and the future just like the past would be present before its eyes."

This notion of pure determinism proved seductive to scientists in various disciplines, a holy grail of sorts that a human intellect, or body of knowledge could, at least theoretically, achieve complete understanding and mastery over not just man's domain, but the universe in total. From our present perspective it also rings as both arrogant and idiotic. For determinism to be true, and eventually realized, free will could not exist. There could be no choice or freedom, nor any notion of randomness.

Other groundbreaking discoveries that furthered the demise of traditional, physics-driven concepts of certainty, include the following:

1   Albert Einstein's theory of relativity demolished the existence of absolute space-time.

2   The uncertainty principle of Werner Heisenberg established that there could be no *absolutely* accurate measurements.

3   Kurt Gödel's incompleteness theorem showed there can be no absolute and final proof.

These discoveries had enormous effects upon the fields of logic and mathematical philosophy. As humankind's understanding expands, so does our capacity to comprehend the *limits* of our understanding. This trajectory continues to accelerate today and manifests in a duality of both astounding insights and baffling new questions; extraordinary technology and the revelation of "impossible" observations; and the coexistence of the quantifiable and the unknowable.

Within this enormous, complex world and the pursuit of truth, knowledge, and beauty, there seems to be plenty of room for both philosophy and science. Faith and fact. Mystery and mastery. I wrote this book to help you rise above the noise of negativity and hollow claims of "certain" predictions to intentionally create more of what is both desirable and unknowable. To do that, thankfully, you need not know everything. You must embrace and do one thing.

One Thing That Changes Everything

As I work with clients, delivering speeches and providing executive and group coaching, I often ask: What is the *one* action you could take or change that would, effectively, change everything? It's amazing how when you seriously consider that question, whether relating it to your job, health, relationships, or a specific challenge, the answer surfaces. Usually, it comes quite quickly. On a conscious or subconscious level, we generally know the answer.

But most people approach chaos and uncertainty from the other direction. They try to intellectually understand it all, then anticipate an exact pathway. They ask, "Considering everything that is happening, all at once, and that which is known and unknown, what should we do?" This approach tends to induce paralysis by analysis instead of action and stems from a deterministic point of view. There is a presupposition that we can somehow gather enough data, expertly analyze it, weigh all potential options and probabilities, and discern the right answer. This also assumes that by the time you get through the process of analysis and discernment, the variables haven't changed requiring you to start over! You can see the inherent problem with this approach, especially given the speed of life, business, and change.

Dynamic systems, such as your life and business, must harmonize determinism (going after what you want) with uncertainty and randomness (dealing with what is). In my view, the best way to do this is to play offense instead of defense. Rather than seeing yourself combating chaos (seeking to subdue or control change, triumph, and restore order), you must become a creator of Positive Chaos.

You are an instrument of change. You devise and detonate intentional forces which may begin small and will amplify in profound, yet unknowable ways. Remember Lorenz's conclusion: small, almost imperceptible changes to the inputs produce huge variations over time.

What are your inputs? Well, quite simply, they include your thoughts, words, and actions: how you process your environment, how you characterize it with language, internally and externally, and how you respond. That's the totality of your "input control"! So, here are the questions to ask yourself: "Are my inputs on autopilot? Am I in perpetual 'reaction mode'? Or am I crafting intentional, elevated, responsive inputs?"

In the second part of this book I will guide you through five transformations that will radically improve your inputs and response system. But before we get there, let's learn to recognize the difference between randomness and uncertainty, and how you can use both to your advantage.

SKILLSET EXERCISE
A POSITIVE MINDSET

Here are some questions that will help you evaluate your current inputs so you can look for the one thing that changes everything.

1   Do you want to learn? What, specifically, do you want to learn? How willing are you to invest yourself and dedicate your capacity to learning?

2   What is the one shift in thinking you can make that will change everything about the way you see your world?

3   How can you change your internal dialogue with yourself and your external dialogue with others to transform the inputs of language?

4   What is the *one* action you can take to

- dramatically improve your professional excellence?
- repair a broken relationship?
- improve your health?
- renew your spirit?
- propel your interests and passions?

4

The Spectrum
of Certainty

I T WAS AUGUST 17, 2019, a Saturday afternoon, when Maggie asked me, "Dad, will you make a TikTok with me?" We went into the back yard and proceeded to dance. Now, I have some moves, and I applied myself fully to the challenge. We were happy with the results, and it was so fun. So random. So us. Maggie posted the video, and we went to the gym to work out. By the time we got back home, that video had hundreds of thousands of views and likes, and an ever-growing assortment of comments. Some were hilarious! We had officially gone viral.

As of this moment, that single video has 26.5 million views, 3.8 million likes, and almost 19,000 comments. That one video was the start of a journey filled with uncertainty and randomness. While Maggie produced her own content, we also continued to post more dances, comedy sketches, pranks, and fun challenges. We experimented, played, and phased in our family's unusual circus skills to keep the audience guessing. One very popular recurring series features the two of us asking each other questions about our lives, testing how much we each know about one another. If one of us gets an answer wrong, the other pushes them into the pool, fully clothed, even when the water's freezing cold in winter!

Maggie's list of followers quickly grew into the hundreds of thousands and then into the millions. The impact of that one video and her single question, "Dad, will you make a TikTok with me?" were significant inputs for the chaos to come. Maggie's career trajectory blossomed into both brand deals and acting, the creation of a worldwide audience, and our family podcast called *Mags and Dad's Wholesome Chaos*. And still new opportunities continue to appear in our lives (mostly hers) with regularity.

The question I wonder about is how much of this journey was random. For whatever reason, we caught the TikTok algorithm at a moment when the app was gaining tremendous popularity but did not have an overflowing number of creators. Maggie's intuition to make that video was a moment of random serendipity. Getting lucky plays its role, for sure.

However, I'm also confident that much of the explosive growth and success that followed was uncertain even though it was driven by intention. Maggie had a clear idea and vision for our videos. We were intentional in how we presented ourselves and our relationship. We tried our best, but didn't take ourselves too seriously. Just a dad and his daughter, having fun, in the spirit of loving play. Because of that, there was a powerful response. In terms of capitalizing on the viral video, or random happenstance, Maggie gets full credit for her innate talent and keen awareness for connecting with her audience. She also has an incredible work ethic and commitment to positive content and high quality. She consistently stacks the odds in her favor—and obviously has a knack for Positive Chaos!

IN BOTH theoretical and practical ways, the study of chaos theory seeks to reconcile the deliberate with the chaotic. In your life, you are doing this too. You are looking to reconcile what you desire and want to pursue (the WAC Model) with that which is uncertain or random in your life. But there's an important distinction to be made here: Is the chaos you're currently experiencing uncertain or random? Although these ideas are often blended in our thoughts, experience, and language, *uncertain* and *random* have different meanings.

Uncertain: not known or definite, in doubt, or presently unknowable.

Random: governed by chance; made, done, or happening without method or conscious decision.

Your experience of uncertainty in life may feel completely random, as if it has no specific cause or origin, but that may not be the case at all. Just because you don't see it coming, doesn't mean it is happenstance. You may be unknowingly swept up in someone else's determinism. Other times, what feels deeply personal and intentional to you is completely random. Understanding the distinction between these two notions will help you map and travel your way through the world, adjusting your expectations and your approach to the situation at hand.

There's a lot about the future that is uncertain and unknowable, as it's still playing out. Will your team win the big game? That answer won't be decided randomly. A process is at work, rules and officials are in place, and teams of participants (players and coaches) are working together to shape the outcomes. Chance plays a role, but it's not the central character.

Will you get a job in the field of your preference? It's uncertain. You shape what happens, and other factors are at work. You handle this by preparing a résumé, filling out applications, networking, interviewing, maintaining momentum, and continuing to improve your skills. You take your shots when you have them and learn from what works and what doesn't.

Randomness is totally different, and life is full of random occurrences, good and bad. They're not connected to logic or determined effort, but just seem to happen out of the blue. How you handle randomness says a lot about you. Are you easily thrown by it? Do you take it personally? Do you give up easily? Or do you find it amusing, validating, and part of life's adventure?

Let's learn how to discern the uncertain from the random, and I will offer you some strategies to address both circumstances.

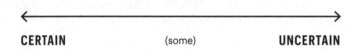

SPECTRUM OF CERTAINTY

CERTAIN   (some)   UNCERTAIN

Uncertainty

Life and uncertainty are synonymous. The sooner you grasp and accept that idea, the sooner you'll be liberated from fear of the unknown and free to fully participate in the unfolding of what's next. The key to forward progress in life is acting, even without full knowledge. This is also the essence of strong leadership.

All you ever get is *some* certainty. This doesn't mean that you're unintelligent or uninformed but rather that you simply cannot know what the events of the future and results of present-day decisions (or indecision) will be. They are unknowable.

I like that word, *unknowable*, because it is both precise and liberating. During the massive disruptions of the COVID pandemic, it's amazing to me how much energy was expended attempting to predict how events would play out. Experts on television, leaders of organizations, and people from all walks of life raced to comment, predict, and project their expectations about what was going to happen. But the problem was we did not have the experience or information to make accurate predictions. No one fully understood the complexity of the situation, but that didn't stop them from saying things.

Early on, many of my speaker colleagues jumped into public forums extolling their predictions and recommendations, and suggesting timelines for what was then just beginning. Now these are very smart people, colleagues I respect greatly. Yet the simple fact was no one knew exactly what was coming, or how long it would last. And on some level, everyone knew that no one knew! So, while there will always be an audience for those who project certainty, and I suppose confidence brings some comfort even if uninformed, those predictions and recommendations rang hollow (or at least unfounded) to me.

Leading in times of chaos requires you to rise above how others respond. Sometimes that means being able to sit comfortably in what is unknowable, even while others freak out completely or demand nonexistent answers. You can do this by mastering three strategies to manage your spectrum of certainty.

Strategy #1: Claim Your Certainties

Even during chaos and confusion, there is much you can know for certain. You know who you are, where you've been, and what you've been through. You have developed valuable insights, skills, and beliefs. You know what you love and who you love. You've learned valuable lessons through intentional pursuits, as well as life's detours, successes and failures, joys and hardships, loves and losses.

Just as Lorenz's attractor model (seen in Chapter 3) featured infinite loops repeating on various planes, it's critical you understand that most of life's challenges are not entirely unprecedented. They are new versions of repeating patterns showing up in various slices of reality. How you handle anything you encounter matters. "Simple" decisions aren't always that simple. Because life presents recurring patterns, the choices you make today will become tomorrow's precedents. The ways you view yourself and engage with your world dramatically affect your future outcomes and behaviors.

When you find yourself in a chaotic situation, ask yourself these questions:

- How is this similar in some ways to what I've already seen or experienced?

- What is it about this moment that is not unprecedented, but actually quite familiar?

- How have I responded in the past to similar situations?

- Was that past response useful and beneficial? If so, how can I repurpose that experience here?

- Or, did I make a mistake and learn a valuable lesson from that response? How can I apply that lesson now?

Separate hard and soft trends

Daniel Burrus, who wrote the foreword to this book, has made accurate predictions about the future for more than four decades. How does he do that? Daniel is the creator of the Burrus Hard Trend Methodology, which separates all trends into one of two categories. They are either *hard trends* or *soft trends*.

Hard trends are based in future facts—things that *will* happen. For example: after 5G wireless, we will get 6G, followed by 7G; AI will continue to grow exponentially more powerful; and baby boomers, along with every other generation, will get older. Hard trends help you identify many disruptions before they happen, turning disruption into a choice. They also let you predict problems and solve them before they happen. Soft trends are based on assumptions that *might* happen, which are also useful because if you don't like a soft trend, you might be able to change it.

Daniel's books, systems, articles, speeches, and consulting have helped countless leaders and their teams separate what *might* be from what *will* be, with a level of certainty that gives them the confidence to make bold moves. With this ability, you are better positioned to manage finite capacity of thought, money, and problem-solving resources, while keeping emotions like fear and anxiety from getting the better of you. When you are feeling completely out of your element or unsure of what's next, claiming your certainties gives you a foundation on which to stand and a perspective to apply going forward.

The irreversibility principle

What's stopping you from pursuing your dreams, creating your success, and gaining greater significance? For so many the barrier is an inability to reconcile past decisions or events with what happens next. To get past your past and on with your journey, I suggest you fully embrace the certainty offered by the irreversibility principle.

The scientific concept of irreversibility refers to processes or reactions that cannot be undone or retraced to their origins. Once you mix two cans of paint, for example, you cannot unmix them. A car once crashed cannot be un-crashed. You can have it repaired, but that car will forever be different. Weakness in structure. Paint marks or layers. You get the drift.

In your life, this principle reigns supreme. You cannot undo past decisions and hardships, un-speak words, or un-harm loved ones. The desperate fantasy that you can undo these actions only produces resentment, self-punishment, and sadness. It also prevents you from taking ownership of what comes next.

Life goes one way—forward. The irreversibility principle liberates you from the past once you understand that everything that happened and is happening now serves you. Now is the time for you to learn and apply the lessons and resolve to change the patterns you've created. You can repair damaged relationships while understanding they will always be different in some ways. Accept this, forgive others, forgive yourself, and move on.

Once you truly embrace irreversibility, you'll see your options more clearly. You can release guilt and resentment, let go of mistakes and missed opportunities, and take responsibility for transforming your reality. You may also be able to see the advantages and opportunities created by what cannot be undone.

Strategy #2: Embrace the Unknown

Your life is an incredible story, taking place in real time. Do you experience it that way? Imagine if you couldn't enjoy a great book or captivating movie unless you knew the ending in advance. Ridiculous, right? When immersed in a great story or adventure, we suspend our need to know and willingly go along for the ride, invested and hopeful, yet ever curious for how the next scene will play out. In fact, we don't even want to know. No spoilers, please! Yet this is not how most people view their lives. Without some assurance about how something will turn out, they are unwilling to start. Without a guarantee of success, they are reluctant to try. As a result, it is difficult for them to fully enjoy or shape their story.

Certainty can only be attained looking backward because your future is unknowable. You may have plans, dreams, and goals. Indeed, a compelling future vision is essential to navigating change, living with joy, and creating Positive Chaos. Rather than seeing your life as uncertain or unknown, I'd suggest you see it as *unfolding*. You are, all at once, the hero at the center of your story, the cocreator of the story, and the enthusiastic spectator watching events unfold. You have a front row seat in the epic tale of your life, and each day you get to contribute dialogue, action, and new plot twists. However, you don't get to write out all the hardships, disasters, unexpected surprises, and contributions of other characters. You incorporate those as you go. Here are a couple of ways to do that.

Deploy play

As children, we learn to model our world, build relationships, resolve conflict, and solve complex problems all within the context of play. Yet as we get older, we may lose connection with this powerful mechanism for growth and achievement.

When life gets confusing and intense, and there's a lot at stake, you may tend to tighten up and get super serious. But there's a better way to bring out your best while embracing the unknown: redeploy your spirit of play in work and life. That could mean taking a break to engage in something fun and energizing. And it also means approaching your work and uncertainty with a more playful attitude, not to diminish the importance of your work, but to reveal new possibilities. Quality output and creativity are byproducts of engagement and momentum. So when you're stuck or feeling tight, a looser, more freeing approach may bring you the needed breakthrough. Here are some ways deploying play may manifest in your own life:

- entertaining new ideas and multiple "right answers."

- trying things you haven't done before.

- doing what you enjoy and are great at.

- being more fully present.

- rising above the seriousness of the moment.

- not just thinking, but actually doing, trying, and discovering what doesn't work and, eventually, what does.

If someone kicks you a ball, literally or metaphorically, you don't take the ball, study it, and put it in a place for safekeeping. You kick it. You take your turn. Are you taking your turn and contributing to the momentum and spirit of the moment? Don't wait for certainty. Open up to the possibilities, act with purpose, trust in yourself, and play.

When you approach life and challenges in fun, you function at a higher level and help others excel. Professional athletes know that in high-stakes competition, staying loose is the key—playing like it doesn't matter when it matters the most. When you bring more play to your everyday, uncertain moments, you distance yourself from negativity while contributing more fully. So, bring more playtime into your work time and throughout your lifetime.

Embrace the law of impermanence

The key to embracing the unknown comes down to a single word: *curiosity*. To stay curious means asking, "What can I learn here? What's this all about? What will happen next?" But it also means accepting that what is now is not forever.

In Buddhism, the *law of impermanence* is a central tenet of understanding that nothing lasts forever, including you. However, you need not practice the faith to grasp the importance and truth of this reality. Everything changes constantly, but many of us act as if it shouldn't. We strive to protect what was, or is, and keep it that way. But history tells us that all civilizations change and transform.

Structures and institutions rise and fall, systems expand, contract, change, and collapse, giving way to new ones.

Coming to grips with impermanence in your own life is essential to finding peace and clarity about what matters, what doesn't, and what to do. Embrace uncertainty and act with purpose. In that way you activate the third strategy.

Strategy #3: Create More Certainty

You create more certainty when you take complete ownership of your circumstances and act in the present moment to shape what is happening. There are two primary ways you create more certainty: challenge yourself, and prioritize your desired future. These are both further examples of what you already know: little things change everything and can transform your personal experience for the better.

When in doubt, challenge yourself

The first way you create more certainty is by creating an intentional, self-imposed challenge in the midst of chaos. You accept the reality of what's happening—your role and responsibility—and you use uncertainty as a catalyst to improve yourself or your environment. It's like saying, "I don't know how this will play out, but however it does, I'll be better in some or many ways."

This may mean learning a new skill or subject, completing a project, or investing time to develop a future work product (such as this book you hold in your hand). There is always an intentional learning opportunity, even when chaos is thrust upon you. Understanding this gives you back some certainty while you simultaneously embrace what's out of your control.

Prioritize your desired future

You also create more certainty by acting in the present with the future in mind. Who are the people you want to be close to later in life? How you treat those people, how you communicate and stay engaged with them now, will go a long way toward solidifying the certainty of your future relationship. Do you desire a future of financial security? If so, are you learning about money, spending less than you make, saving, and investing for retirement? Even if these efforts are minimal, you can have more certainty knowing you'll likely be in a better financial position later that offers more options, fewer hardships, and an improved quality of life.

Randomness

In March 2005, I was part of a four-man team of performers delivering entertainment and encouragement to troops deployed in the Iraq War. Our Chinook helicopter had just touched down in Ramadi, Iraq, well after midnight. We flew at night to reduce the probability of enemy gunfire, traveling between US bases in our month-long tour. This was week three, and we had been steadily working our way downrange—that is, we were moving closer to the active fighting. By this time, we were at the front lines. As we walked in the dark toward our pods (small, mobile sleeping units), where we would spend the short remainder of the night, we passed a sizable gaping hole in the dirt not more than fifty yards from our accommodations.

"See that?" our host, Major Ron Tootle of the US Marines, asked. "That's the crater from a mortar round last week that came in over the wall."

"Should we be worried about that?" I asked.

"Nah," he answered. "Occasionally they shoot rounds at the base, but they're not really aiming at anything specific. We look at mortar rounds like lightning strikes. They're totally random, and the odds of one hitting you is pretty low. So we don't worry about it. We just live with it."

Somehow, that explanation gave me comfort, and as I was also completely exhausted, I had no problem sinking into a deep night's sleep.

Randomness, chance, and probabilities exist in our world. These work both to our benefit and detriment. Fortune and opportunity may strike when you least expect it, and because of no "method or conscious decision" on your part. Tragedy and hardship can also happen without fault, justification, or warning. I knew a woman who was riding a bicycle through a park on a perfectly sunny day when a tree gave way and fell, striking her as she was moving and leaving her paralyzed. Some would call this fate, others bad timing. Without a doubt, that incident was extraordinarily random. Now, having heard this story, how would you react or approach future opportunities of spending time around trees?

You live and work on a playing field (phase space) where you make deliberate, determined moves, and confront random obstacles and opportunities. This is part of the excitement of life. Humans love to play games. From when we first discover peekaboo as babies, we are hooked by both the predictability and the randomness of what's to come. The best games share elements of both strategy and chance. If it's all about luck, many of us lose interest. Although strategy alone can be engaging, such as in puzzle solving and theoretical plans, it's still incomplete. It leaves out chance encounters that require you to adapt. But the game of life and enterprise of business are all about executing strategy while adapting to what randomly happens, so here are three strategies to use when faced with randomness.

Strategy #1: Understand Probability

When faced with a situation that seems promising or risky, it's easy for us to exaggerate the potential upside or the potential disaster. We can talk ourselves into investments or plans by inflating the likelihood of huge payoffs. And we can also talk ourselves out of meaningful pursuits and opportunities by exaggerating the risks. Instead, try to see randomness in its actual relationship to probability.

For instance, many people are absolutely fearful of speaking in front of an audience. When given an opportunity to address a professional group or a gathering of peers within their community, they would likely decline it, even if they had something important or meaningful to say. Why? They perceive the risk to be enormous: public humiliation, rejection, personal defeat, and extreme discomfort before, during, and after the talk.

However, I can tell you with confidence, as someone who speaks professionally and mentors other speakers and executives through this process, those risks are highly inflated. In truth, audiences are not adversaries but allies—they are on your side. They want you to be real, relaxed, and natural. In other words, the less you try to impress them, the more connected they feel to you. As those in your audience are also most likely fearful of speaking, they will give you the benefit of the doubt and extend understanding if things don't go perfectly. In fact, the less-than-perfect moments endear you to them provided you take them in stride. So, the imagined risks are out of proportion to reality. And also, the likely upside is undervalued.

This courageous act of Positive Chaos, saying yes to something that initially scares you, could potentially transform your confidence, as well as your connection to many others. What you share could impact their lives or expand their knowledge, and it changes the way they see and value you as a person, teammate, or leader. The probability of the downside is far lower than is the positive upside potential.

Strategy #2: Increase the Odds

Although you cannot eliminate negative random possibilities, you can reduce them. You cannot guarantee success, but you can certainly increase the odds of it through preparation and education or by aligning with the advice of experts or taking proven courses of action.

In our example, you will plan your speaking remarks, rather than just winging it. You'll organize your thoughts, points, and stories in order to make your case or deliver a desired message. Rather than scripting your presentation word for word, I'd suggest creating a strong outline. You may talk with others to get input on both the content and the process of delivering your speech. You'll do some rehearsals to get a sense of timing, perhaps, or prepare a slide deck. Whatever it takes to help you feel ready, prepared, and as confident as you can be, given the fact that the ultimate outcome is unknowable.

Strategy #3: When Lightning Strikes, Don't Take It Personally

Consider all random occurrences as part of the unknowable story of life. When fortune smiles upon you, it doesn't mean you're a genius. When hardship randomly strikes, it isn't that you did something wrong—it's probably not about you at all. Interpret randomness as the hand you are dealt at that moment, and realize that you always have the next move.

You show up for speech day prepared, yet also nervous. In fact, you feel a buzz of energy inside your body. This is normal and necessary to help you focus, and also a great indication that this moment means something to you. Somehow, you distract yourself and breathe through the discomfort, remembering that you are ready. You have nothing to prove, just something to share. And as you do, random elements will strike. Expect them. These may be brilliant insights you share, spontaneous moments that result in laughter, or periods of distraction when you felt disengaged from the audience. Eventually the experience ends, and now suddenly you realize you've not only survived it, but you've enjoyed it. And the audience did too! They're asking you questions and offering compliments. Some of that, invariably, relates to the idea that you are brave and admired. They tell you, "I could never do that." By now, however, you realize it really wasn't that big a deal. Actually, at least for the moment, you want to do it again.

AS A PRACTITIONER of Positive Chaos, you are now on a journey to capitalize on fortuitous opportunities while shrugging off the randomness that detracts. None of it is about you, but it can almost always serve you in some way. You claim that belief with certainty, leveraging your irreversible past. Then you embrace the unknown, and self-prescribe a continuous curriculum to grow through the changes.

Now, we turn our attention to recognize the primary contributor to your state of chaos. Let's simplify complexity.

5

Complexity Simplified

Y OU WAKE UP with good intentions and a plan of action. The day is full of promise and possibility. It starts simply, with items and tasks prioritized in your mind, on your device, or scribbled on a to-do list. And then you start interacting with the world and complexity bombards you. First, it's the phone. All you wanted to do was turn off the alarm and take a quick look at your email, just to see if you got an anticipated reply. Immediately, you are confronted by other people's agendas: spam (which you delete for satisfaction) and other requests and demands for your time and attention. You realize you'll need to spend some time on this later, but already you find your brain divided and are feeling behind the wave of activity, rather than surfing daybreak.

After putting down the phone, you encounter the people, pets, or problems in your immediate environment. Trying to keep momentum, you take care of what's required as you get dressed, fed, and properly caffeinated. Waiting for the coffee, you take another look at the phone and this time find yourself reflexively opening your favorite social media app. Instantly, you're drawn into images, videos, and words you never expected. Each flick of the thumb opens a window into someone else's world, problems, or creativity. It's as if you have outsourced your intention and thoughts, which, you recognize in a few minutes, is the opposite of what you need to do. Still, the dopamine rush was a nice complement to the coffee.

Now you are getting organized and making your morning commute, whether that's to your in-home office or across town. By the time you're ready to focus, attempting to recapture earlier clarity and intentions, you realize you have more email, requests, and that reply you were waiting on isn't what you hoped for. Problems you never anticipated require solving, or at least addressing, before you can make meaningful progress. And just like that, before you've really even started, complexity has once again fragmented your thinking, stalled your progress, and discouraged your hopeful ambition.

This all-too-common story illuminates what you now understand; complexity and chaos are directly related. The more complex a system or circumstance, and the more open it is to outside influence, the greater the likelihood that chaos exists. But exactly where does this complexity come from? What motivates it? And how can leaders and other humans operate in complex environments without becoming distracted, discouraged, and overwhelmed by debilitating chaos? This chapter will offer those answers.

WE SEE complexity as negative when it impedes our efforts or we are attempting to predict an outcome. But you can only anticipate or guide; you never fully control the inputs and motivations of other people. Therefore, maintaining order and certainty in complex systems is immensely challenging, if even possible. If maintaining order and certainty is the challenge you've signed up for in your life, you will be perpetually frustrated and perplexed. And here's the sneaky secret: that's exactly the intention of those who would deliberately use complexity to influence your behavior or seek to diminish your efforts.

However, if you adopt the mindset and methods of Positive Chaos, you understand that within the system you directly influence—your own life—everything you engage with carries the imprint of your intention. How you manage your morning sets the intention for your entire day. The way you speak with your spouse or children informs the conversations to come with clients and customers. What you notice, value, and prioritize in the moments between tasks positions you differently for what's to come and changes the scope of your available options. In short, everything affects everything.

This interconnectedness of all that you experience and influence contains both complexity and synergy (which I will cover in more depth in Chapter 12). When you begin to see the aspects of your life not as separate or competing but as connected and collaborating, you can use complexity to your advantage. Understanding the nature and intention of the complexity coming at you helps you formulate your approach and set your expectations. But there are different forms of complexity to understand and anticipate.

THREE TYPES OF COMPLEXITY

Which type of complexity currently occupies the
majority of your time, focus, and energy?

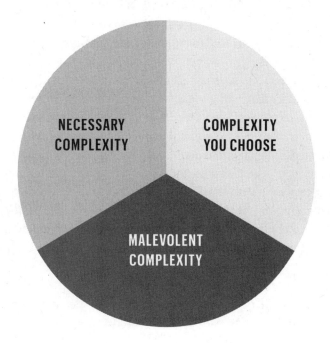

NECESSARY COMPLEXITY

COMPLEXITY YOU CHOOSE

MALEVOLENT COMPLEXITY

Necessary Complexity

Big problems are rarely as easy to solve as you initially think, and complex skills or jobs can look far easier than they actually are. Take, for example, my chosen profession as a speaker, author, and performance coach. While I enthusiastically advocate (as I did last chapter) that everyone consider speaking in front of an audience, to make this your vocation is an entirely different undertaking.

When I'm presenting onstage at conferences, performing at my best, it may seem easy to those in my audience. That ease and effortlessness, honed through decades of experience, can inspire many people to think, "I'd like to do that too!" And they probably can, on some level, and in their own way, but they don't yet fully understand the complex challenges of the assignment.

At the National Speakers Association, where I have served as president, we have a steady churn of new members. The seductive appeal of the speaking profession, plus the fact that it seems so easy—*You just get on stage and talk in a persuasive, engaging way. I'm persuasive. I'm engaging. I know how to talk!*—has people showing up eager and excited to NSA meetings, asking, "Where do I get speeches?"

Because the business is necessarily complex, the answer is far more complicated than typically expected. It goes something like this: "Public speaking is a fantastic profession. First, there's a lot about *presenting* that you need to learn, such as crafting your speeches, delivery, story structure, and connecting with an audience using humor, as well as intellect. You need to find the intersection of your expertise with the audience's problem so that your content is absolutely *relevant* to their needs. You also need to learn the business side, including marketing, branding, website development, and sales. You need a video that shows your work at its best, on stage in front of a live audience. However, right now you don't yet have a speech . . . or an audience, so that's a challenge. But if you create the right content and position it properly, you may attract the attention of clients and meeting planners. If you have the skills and content, this whole journey usually takes five to ten years before you're established in the profession, although some do achieve success faster."

For many would-be speakers, when the reality of the necessary complexity of the process strikes them, the limitations of willingness kick in. Some people will be completely energized about the process, and others will be fully discouraged before they even start.

SOME COMPLEX problems are far more serious and complicated. Take, for example, the incredible challenges currently facing American schoolchildren, including increasing suicide rates in teens, other mental health issues, and terror and anxiety created by mass shootings. These are heartbreaking issues in need of urgent attention. When we hear the statistics, or when a violent episode hits the news, our immediate outcry of horror and intolerance is absolutely understandable. The natural response is *We must do something now!* And many people *are* doing something, including my client JP Guilbault, CEO of Navigate360. You'll learn more about JP and his leadership philosophy later in the book.

Navigate360 is a mission-driven organization whose purpose is to empower people, schools, and communities to stay safe and thrive physically, socially, and emotionally. They offer products, training, resources, and thought leadership in three areas: threat detection and prevention, mental health and wellness, and safety management and preparedness. They believe that teen suicide and violence are preventable in a high percentage of cases *if* holistic solutions are in place and the proper capabilities and awareness are cultivated. The company's response to such challenges is far more comprehensive than the simple soundbites we hear that drive our outrage.

I interviewed JP soon after the horrific school shooting in Uvalde, Texas, and asked him if he found it frustrating that people seek to reduce these complex issues to simple solutions or political stances. This is what he said.

> You hit it on the head ... it was frustrating to see how quickly and predictably this turned into a gun policy debate ... It's actually really

complex and ... the answer lies in a multi-threaded approach ... One, we have to raise the level of awareness and education in society to people in need, and to the behaviors that signal there is a potential for harm. Next, we need a multidisciplinary approach to assessing threats in communities and schools. Third is intervention. We must have a way in which counseling mental illness expands beyond the clinical diagnosis and how you address and care for the systemic problem of homicidal and suicidal behavior. And lastly, we do need common sense gun policy—and an honest conversation about what that means. We are at an inflection point in my mind as a country. The degradation of the family and faith-based units where values and virtues were instilled in youth character and the role-modeling of division and social aggression on display by political leaders are accelerating the hopelessness and apathy of our youth.

If you honestly want to face and solve a problem, especially a necessarily complex problem, you must first wrap your mind completely around it. Only then can you remove the noise from the necessary work and figure out strategies for solutions.

The Complexity You Choose

Complexity is an inherent and necessary element of dynamic systems. However, when you choose to inject additional complexity into a system, you also create exponentially greater chaos. We can do this consciously to create something new, enact a desire, or aspire to higher standards. We also make unconscious, reflexive choices that invite less desirable complications into our lives. And the butterfly effect means that it doesn't take much to push an already complex but functioning system into chaotic disorder. Here's a lighthearted example of when choosing to add complexity created some unintended results.

Disc golf is rapidly gaining in nationwide popularity. It is played on courses at parks and campuses, which are usually free. The goal is to throw various discs (think Frisbees but designed for specific flight characteristics and longer distances) from the tee boxes, around obstacles, and into elevated baskets made of hanging chains, which are designed to catch an accurate throw with a triumphant "Cha-ching!"

I love this sport as it speaks to my kinesthetic passions. It also incorporates both determinism (skill and strategy) and chaotic randomness (wind gusts or odd bounces that may help or hinder you at any moment). Plus, it's a great chance to spend time with both human and canine friends. I have a regular weekly game with my friends Lee and Wayne, along with our collective five dogs, two of which, Simon and Spencer, belong to me. The dogs love it. In fact, I'd say other than my wife, it's their favorite thing. Because of the secluded nature of the course, they get to run off-leash much of the time. They have come to know each other and operate in a pack, listening to our cues and instructions. We're responsible and attentive about other golfers, other dogs, and picking up poop. Plus, the dogs get treats at random intervals. All this activity is incorporated into the challenge of playing the course. There's a lot going on, but we've developed and honed a functional system.

One day our friend Tiny (a kind and generous former football player who is anything but his nickname) joined us with his dog, Roxy, who is also super well behaved and mindful of her owner. However, taking our five dogs to a six pack changed the dynamics of the entire operation—complexity skyrocketed. It wasn't just Roxy who injected some chaos, it was each dog's perception and reaction to Roxy, driven by their own personalities and idiosyncrasies. Add Roxy's curiosity about each of us humans, and that she didn't yet know the rules of the situation she found herself in, and we were in chaos. For the first few holes, we found ourselves tripping over dogs, correcting unpredictable behavior, and spending more time herding animals than playing disc golf! Roxy (smart girl) figured it out though. Within twenty minutes, she was incorporated into the pack, and we were once again in a functional groove.

Let this story remind you: As you choose to incorporate additional complexity into your life or business, understand that it will create both predictable and unpredictable results. Anticipate what you can, but expect and prepare for surprise. Learn quickly and make real-time adjustments. And please, pick up the poop. Now, let's shift from the lighthearted to a more serious view of complexity's impact and get some expert advice on how you can become a more critical thinker.

More Than You Can Handle

Ellen McCarthy is not a spy, but she has worked with spies regularly. Serving in the US Intelligence Community for more than thirty years, and eventually as the assistant to the secretary of state for the Bureau of Intelligence and Research, Ellen understands the challenge of managing vast amounts of complex information in the search for what is accurate and useful.

"I started as a Soviet submarine analyst," she told me. "Think *Hunt for Red October*. The information we had was driven by spies on the ground and satellites in the air. I had access to a tight set of the best data. That is not the case today. Now, there is so much more data available in the private sector, some of which is accurate. So the job of the intelligence agencies is actually much harder than it used to be because you have to get through all the bad data to find the truth."

According to Ellen, "This very negative thing is also a positive. As a global order, we've produced more information in the past two years than in all of previous human history. And part of the challenge is physiological. Our brains are simply not wired to absorb and categorize so much information. To cope with this, we shut down and just look for the information that confirms our existing view of the world."

You'll hear more from Ellen in future chapters, including in Chapter 16 on leading through chaos. For now, however, use this expert opinion to give yourself some slack while you also consider your sources. You cannot be productive with all the information. If trained intelligence analysts with enormous budgets, teams, and technology are struggling to discern what's going on, perhaps this can put your own challenges in perspective. Yet, if you are only confirming what you think you already know, are you thinking critically?

"Anyone can become a more critical thinker," Ellen said, before offering these three helpful suggestions:

1 If you're experiencing an emotional reaction, don't respond. Pause and breathe until you can calm yourself and see things more objectively.

2 Don't immediately discount things that appear outlandish. Even in what initially seems absurd, there is often a hint of truth.

3 Instead of isolated incidents, look for repeated patterns.

Malevolent Complexity

Have you ever had to wait on hold for an hour to resolve a complaint, or found yourself at a dead-end on self-navigated hold menus, wondering why it is so hard to just cancel a subscription?

A 2019 *Harvard Business Review* article called "Why Is Customer Service So Bad? Because It's Profitable" states that the average American spends thirteen hours on hold each year, one-third of customers require more than one call to resolve a complaint, and many give up after the first attempt. The authors of that article wrote that their "research suggests that some companies may actually find it profitable to create hassles for complaining customers, even if it were to operationally cost less not to." Those companies aim to disincentivize the behaviors they want to discourage (like cancelling a subscription) by making those behaviors more difficult and time-consuming.

Although this is a scary scenario, it does make perfect sense and answers the question, "Why do they make this so complicated?" If you have ever found yourself in this situation, it is likely that one of three underlying motivations are fueling the mayhem.

You may be dealing with incompetence. The organizers or operators of a system are working beyond the scope of their abilities, capacity, and understanding, and they are overwhelmed. This can be addressed with training, coaching, additional staffing, or technological support.

Or you may be dealing with unnecessary complexity. Over time, benevolent participants and leaders add unnecessary complexity in the form of ad hoc solutions to address situational problems in a systemic way. These solutions may not play well together, though, and result in a dysfunctional or at least clunky experience. In this situation, you need to streamline system design and remove unnecessary complexity.

And finally, there may be malevolent complexity at work, the kind exhibited by companies who want to make it hard for you to cancel their services. But this kind of complexity can be far more serious than that. Because complexity is incredibly disruptive to a system, it can be weaponized to intentionally overwhelm or break a system. Organizations and individuals may intentionally inject complexity designed to create harmful chaos that will destabilize a system, population, or individual. There's nothing random about this. The attractors, or "pulls" on your attention and motivations are, in this case, *detractors*.

Malevolent complexity is an intentional, deterministic objective to cause havoc, overwhelm systems, and make life more complicated. This may sound like conspiracy theory, but it happens every single day in both small and large ways, throughout the world. Governments seek to destabilize one another or control their own populations by creating chaotic complexity.

Another insight from my interview with Ellen McCarthy: "As a country we are more divided than ever. The absence of trust in government and media organizations is as great as it's ever been. As a result, countries like Russia and China can very much take advantage of this weakness. Our openness is our kryptonite. We're vulnerable. There are forces outside our country who are stoking our divisiveness and making us weaker on some level."

Governments, of course, also battle over resources, technology, and economic sanctions and experience complexity through migration of populations fleeing war or seeking new opportunities.

Organized movements and self-motivated individuals set their aims to cripple functional systems they oppose or seek to replace. Political campaigns spend millions on creating attack ads that cause problems for their opponents rather than promoting their own agendas.

Athletes may intentionally confuse their opponents and complicate their ability to function on a playing field. It's part of the playbook! The same is true on the competitive fields of business, where adversaries battle over talent, competitors, suppliers, products, and time to market. We strive to simplify and streamline our progress and success. And if we can complicate things for our competitors, well, that's a bonus!

On social media, a simple tweet, post, or viral video can create incredible complications, causing people, brands, and organizations to go into full-blown defensive mode. This power is often wielded with the intention to harm, hinder, or destroy. When I was president of the National Speakers Association, it was frustrating to see a repeating pattern of how an intentional comment in one of the association's public Facebook groups could immediately hijack the attention of the leadership team and the energy and resources of the organization. The existing pattern was to respond with great care in the context that was established by the attacker, essentially agreeing with the premise. These were often aggressive criticisms of the organization, sometimes swerving into politically charged subjects.

These detractors were, themselves, seeking to gain attention, grow their following, and benefit in reputational or financial gain at the expense of the association they belonged to. These tactics had worked for years, bringing them attention while creating massive disruptions and complexities for the organization. I took bold action to break those patterns by kindly, directly, and publicly calling out the tactic and intention behind the post. I openly provided all context and invited anyone interested in learning more to contact me directly. This approach worked in my situation, quickly defusing the issue and disarming the antagonist.

Don't even get me started on governmental complexity. Why are efforts to simplify our tax code met with huge resistance? Why does the scope of government simultaneously expand and become less efficient? When constant crisis serves those in power by making them more powerful, what is the motivation to transcend crisis, reduce scope, and simplify?

I don't want to encourage you to engage in malevolent complexity by undermining those you disagree with or dislike. That would violate the principle of positivity. It would also perpetuate continued conflict on some level, creating mental and physical consequences you'd have to reconcile with at some point.

Nor do I want you to become cynical, thinking the whole world is out to get you. That simply isn't true. Presume positive.

I do, however, want you to know that malevolent complexity exists. It's out there. You will encounter it, and probably are dealing with it in some ways right now. You can't solve malevolent complexity. Instead, you must find a way to transcend it, avoid it, or call it out (as in my example about dealing with the Facebook posts). Don't take the bait and end up becoming physically and emotionally drained. Play your game and undermine negativity with Positive Chaos.

Keep It Simple

In addition to disc golf, I also enjoy regular golf (or as disc golfers call it, ball golf), both as a player and a spectator. My grandfather introduced me to golf when I was fourteen, and it brings me fond memories of our times together. I love that the sport is an individual test—you against the course. That's why on any given weekend, I'll often turn on the TV to watch golf, especially when a big event, such as one of the four major tournaments (the Masters, British Open, US Open, and PGA Championship) is taking place. I find it relaxing to take in the beautiful scenery and vicariously play the course through the best players in the world. When it comes to the golf interviews, however, my wife and I have a running gag and crack each other up. We sometimes spontaneously enter "interview mode," with one of us playing the part of the golfer who offers up different versions of the same answer to the reporter's questions.

That's because, invariably, before every round, commentators interview the players who are in position to win, asking something like, "Given your current challenges, and last week's results, what's your plan today? You've been working on your swing recently, and do those new changes help you given the way the course is set up? I mean, with the rough as high as it is, and with the wind gusting today, will that play a factor in your strategy?" The questions are always about complexity: Given all that's happening, how will you control the elements and deal with everything?

Among the best players in the world, the answer to these kinds of questions is always a variation of the following: "Yeah, that's all true. But for me, I feel I'm striking it well. I'm just going to play my game; try to make some good swings and hit some fairways off the tee to put myself in position. If I can do that, then I can put the ball on the green. Then, if I can just hit some good putts and stay patient, I can do well today."

What's their answer to complexity? Always, every time, it is some form of simplicity: swings, fairways, greens, putts.

IN THE WORLD of technology sales teams, Chris Stites is a hired gun. He's brought in by CEOs to build world-class sales organizations that can execute, win, and scale up quickly. Chris not only makes an organization profitable, but also extremely valuable and attractive for acquisition. This is the pattern Chris is known for executing, and I asked him to explain his process.

"In sales we live in chaos. Every single deal, buyer, and seller bring uniqueness and complexity. I help salespeople create stability through constantly changing circumstances. We find the three to five things we need to be great at and communicate that over and over. We also celebrate both the victories and the losses, as the deals we don't win teach us something valuable. We make sure everyone learns from everyone else and bring it all right back to the basics."

Whether in sports or sales, the lesson is clear. If you are trying to perform well under pressure in complex, challenging, and dynamic situations, avoid overly complicating your approach. Instead, simplify it to the most essential repeatable actions and ideas. Then execute, learn, and repeat. How can you simplify and focus on the most important, repeatable aspects of your success?

Complexity isn't the enemy, it's the reality. By recognizing its various attributes and challenges, we can also find opportunity in complexity, as you will encounter in our closing skillset exercise. Once you review, learn, and internalize these principles, you will be more capable of managing complexity for yourself and others.

Next, to bolster your resilience and command of Positive Chaos, let's strengthen your personal stability.

SKILLSET EXERCISE
NAVIGATING COMPLEXITY

Problems are complex. Principles are simple. Therefore, applying these principles to navigate complexity helps you bring confidence to confusion and uncertainty.

1 **When seeking deep understanding, look for complexity.** Most problems are more complicated than you think. Every "easy answer" creates unintended consequences. Every upside has a downside, and quite often people who are doing what you perceive to be wrong are motivated by an intention or idea you don't fully understand. Don't jump to conclusions, stretch to understand.

2 **Whenever possible, reduce or remove complexity.** Make that your mantra in leadership and life. If a process can be reduced to fewer steps while maintaining its integrity, do it. If your objective or concept is three pages long, it will be far less compelling than three sentences. Or one. Consistently strive to edit out unnecessary words, steps, and impediments.

3 **In complex situations, elevate your thinking to one simple concept above everything else.** To some this will be seen as "oversimplifying what is complicated." But that's not it. You are discerning the true and useful idea that drives greater clarity for yourself and those around you. Complexity paralyzes you. Simplicity drives useful thought and positive action.

4 **Seek synergy.** Look for connections. Trust that positive complexity exists beyond your understanding *and serves you* when your actions are motivated by true and honorable intentions.

5 **Sidestep the traps of malevolent complexity.** Don't waste your time and power dealing with systems and people that don't have your best interests in mind. Learn to recognize this trap and protect your emotional energy by seeing them for what they are.

6

Stability on
the Move

HOW BEAUTIFULLY poetic (or ironic) that while I've been research-
ing and writing a book on Positive Chaos, my wife and I have
been going through one of the most disruptive, positively chaotic periods of our life together. Our marriage is solid. But
after twenty-two years living in the same house—our kids' child-
hood home—we decided to move to a new house in a different town.
This was a self-imposed (-inflicted) decision: complexity we chose.
And we picked this moment to make it happen. So now, while in the
midst of a busy speaking schedule, out of town travels, promised
commitments to my publisher and oh-so-patient editor (thank you,
Sarah), and my wife's productions as a writer and filmmaker, we are
processing twenty-two years of accumulation and life. Twenty-two
years of deferred decisions, coming due all at once.

This vastly complex process has gone on for months and involved
fixing up and selling two properties in a wildly shifting real estate
market, buying a new house, and incorporating my wife's parents'
estates and belongings into our lives. Multiple moves and storage
units. Endless boxes. Cathartic purges. And still, the work continues.
Now, this experience is not unique to us, of course. Moving is consistently rated among the most stressful experiences in life! I would

concur with that, and while we've been on the move, we've found it imperative to maintain a sense of stability.

As you encounter, confront, and create chaos in your life and in the world, I believe it is possible and necessary to increase personal stability while navigating enormous external instability and change. In this way, not only can you transform your personal experience of chaos from negative to positive—or from reactive to responsive—you can also better serve your loved ones, your team, and the world you live in and influence. In this chapter, I'll help you increase your personal stability, even in the midst of external instability, along your journey through Positive Chaos.

Balance Is What You Do

In my previous book, *Off Balance On Purpose*, I explored how the concept of balance is misunderstood and erroneously pursued as a desirable, future goal. You've probably been told that if you work hard enough, smart enough, or long enough, you'll eventually find order and simplicity and achieve the elusive state of balance. But in truth, balance is never what you get, it's what you do.

Balancing your life is about early recognition of what's happening, deciding what's important, and making adjustments to maintain what is or to move toward your desired outcome. Often, that requires you to go off balance intentionally. You must lean into the challenges or opportunities you face, embrace short-term disruptions, and invite complexity for long-term benefit. In this way you learn to find both deep meaning, or purpose, and the satisfaction of initiating and pursuing a path you own and shape.

In the field of chaos theory, this principle of being off balance on purpose resides in the language of equilibrium and disequilibrium. *Equilibrium* implies a resting state where no changes are occurring. But for something to happen, there must be an imbalance, an attraction, a reaction, or a process happening—*disequilibrium*. Dynamic systems only occur when disequilibrium exists. This is how life operates. To make things happen intentionally, you must maintain stability while creating disequilibrium.

Equilibrium and stability are companions as they both directly relate to the condition of an object or system in the flow of change. A system, an object, or a person can preserve stability while they undergo change. And the more stable, functionally sound, and grounded they are, the easier the person, system, or object can incorporate changes without being completely disrupted. This is crucial to understand when you deploy small changes to your inputs to cause amplified future results.

Instability or disequilibrium can take many forms, both in the world of science and in the "phase space" of life. Scientific categories include chemical instability, hydrostatic instability, hydrodynamic instability, thermodynamic instability, and many other physical forms. In life, however, we also clearly see and understand the impacts of political instability, financial instability, societal instability, family instability, and mental instability.

Instability can lead to positive conditions and provide a precursor to beneficial change. However, a system cannot remain unstable forever. Just as nature passes through moments of equilibrium to find disequilibrium, it uses instability to seek and discover more stable systems.

How to Increase Your Stability in Times of Chaos

Although change can strike at any moment, stability provides protection from negative chaos while connecting you to positive elements you value and influence. What follows are some examples of ways to increase stability in the many spheres of your life.

Finances

Our *Impact of Chaos* study revealed that 65 percent of working Americans considered "Financial Chaos" to be extremely stressful (37 percent) or somewhat stressful (28 percent), making this the most stressful type of chaos experienced, by far. Not having enough money to pay bills today, of course, erodes the stability of your circumstances and psyche. Also, uncertainty of future financial stability plays into our stress levels and fears, regardless of our current situation.

Without a doubt, money provides stability and gives you choices you would otherwise not have. Therefore, creating income and streamlining expenses helps promote stability. But having stable finances isn't only about the money you're making, it's about the money you save and invest to provide psychological and practical assurance that even in desperate times you won't be quite so desperate. Acquiring insurance and using other financial instruments may contribute to your sense of stability.

Family

My family, which includes my wife and children, my parents and sisters, and my extended family of uncles, aunts, and cousins, is the bedrock of my stability. I define success, first and foremost, by how I function and show up for family. It's important to attend reunions, weddings, and funerals; doing so generally takes precedence regardless of what's happening in my own life.

But let's face it, families are complicated. Even within a functional, loving family, which I'm blessed to enjoy, there are incredible complications. Working with your spouse, as I do, invites additional complexity, making some aspects of business easier and others more difficult. Yet, that continuity or stability is so vital and valuable to me. Being there for one another, unconditionally, is what makes life meaningful, and what I know will matter most in the end. If the family you belong to or come from doesn't provide you the stability you desire, well, you may choose to remedy that or create a different pattern.

Friends

Friends are the family you choose. Keep people in your life whom you love, enjoy, and respect; friends who stretch you and emulate the qualities you admire. Your life will reflect, in many ways, the values and characteristics of your closest companions. Choose them carefully and invest yourself in their lives. Prioritizing friends creates stability for times when you'll need support. You may also need to distance yourself from the friends who create instability or undermine your growth.

Faith

Many people, including me, find stability in their spiritual beliefs, or in a faith-based community, and in the perspective that their life is a small component of an eternal story. Here, please understand, I'm not speaking about the *exactness* of God, or a particular ideology. I am alluding to the *existence* of something bigger than you are. Call it what you want. Universal Intelligence. Higher Power. The Force.

During times of chaos, faith can be an especially vital source of strength and comfort, helping you handle what is necessary, endure what is difficult, and do what is needed to help others. Even among the agnostic and atheists, there exists the understanding of virtue and the inherent value of doing what is right. This takes belief—some call it faith—that there is an inherent moral necessity to follow our consciences. It is in the listening to that pull—the internal attractor—that we find additional stability and assurance that our actions are properly motivated.

Health

The healthier you are, mentally and physically, the greater your ability to withstand future hardships. Stability of health can be fragile by nature, and at any moment an unexpected injury, accident, or illness can strike. However, even if that happens, preexisting health is a huge predictor and contributor to rapid recovery.

Skills and education

The more you know and are capable of doing, the greater the likelihood that you will be able to cope with future uncertainty and randomness. Take the time to develop valuable skills continuously; become a lifelong learner, teacher, and contributor to others.

Stability provides confidence to help you take on new complexity, intentional change, and learning. As you move through changes and growth opportunities, it is helpful for you to understand where you currently reside in the process of any new undertaking so that you can anticipate what might be coming next.

Accelerating Through the Curves

When you drive through a curve, you create stability not by slowing down but through controlled acceleration. Applying positive force, within limits, allows better handling and responsiveness. Similarly, Positive Chaos involves continuing to innovate and grow while enjoying success or experiencing change. So how do you make that happen? Let's explore how growth typically works.

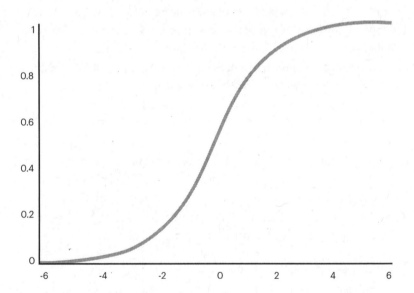

The logistic curve

Growth within any system is represented by a *logistic curve*, also known as a sigmoid curve, or S-curve. Perhaps you've seen this model applied in various ways to discuss growth of businesses, a population, new markets, or the performance thresholds of everything from sales teams to athletes.

Here's what you need to know about growth so that you can recognize when complexity and chaos might take hold. Growth begins slowly at first, requires effort to gain momentum, and then it goes through an exponential rise. But as energy and resources diminish, or thresholds are reached, rapid growth cannot be sustained indefinitely. At that point, the curve flattens. The point at which it flattens, or the upper limit, is called the *asymptote*.

The system starts in a condition of "unstable equilibrium" then changes and grows, slowly at first, then much more quickly. When the curve reaches limitations, or "carrying capacity" near the asymptote, it trends back toward equilibrium. The condition of this new equilibrium, however, is more stable.

Unleashing the Energy of Your Learning Curves

Think of your personal or organizational learning curve as a logistic curve. Initially, you are in a condition of unstable equilibrium. You are sitting on unleashed energy, or unfocused curiosity. You then recognize a learning opportunity or a need within the marketplace. This early recognition creates disequilibrium and launches you on a journey of learning and experimentation.

As you develop a basic understanding of the foundational principles and skills, progress is slow at first. You create systems and processes that make learning more efficient, and soon you begin to experience rapid growth. Your understanding and capabilities rise quickly, which feels fantastic and rewarding; however, learning and growth require far more effort as you find yourself approaching the asymptote. Here, it will take you significantly more resources and time to achieve more gains.

This growth pattern plays out regularly within organizations. When the organization is enjoying the gains and rewards of early efforts (increased sales, market share, new customers, and the momentum of having innovated), leaders and teams are often slow to realize the approach of limiting factors (diminished resources, new competitors, or the aging of innovation). Maintaining the growth or results that the organization has grown accustomed to suddenly seems impossible or requires a disproportionate and expensive investment of time, resources, and human effort. The trick to avoid stalling out here is looking ahead to see where you can jumpstart another learning curve.

Harnessing Momentum with Consecutive Curves

For both people and organizations, sustaining growth requires identifying and embarking upon new learning and growth opportunities while still experiencing the rise of the current logistic curve. In other words, you don't wait for your present S-curve to lose steam, you look for adjacent curves—new learning and growth opportunities—and you deploy personal and organizational effort to create a new curve, simultaneously. You use momentum to your advantage.

With this strategy, as the current system, project, or business segment approaches its limitations, requiring more effort and growing more slowly, the new curve, ideally, is finding traction and moving into the phase of acceleration.

Positive Chaos involves continuing to innovate while enjoying success. Remaining a beginner while becoming an expert. Staying curious and open to new and better answers, instead of getting stuck in proven strategies. As you come into your power as an instrument for positive disruption, you'll become disenchanted with equilibrium and intrigued by disruption and change. You're not disillusioned. You're fully aware that the future is uncertain, unfolding, and, in many respects, unknowable. You know that randomness plays a role and must be incorporated along the way. Yet you also realize

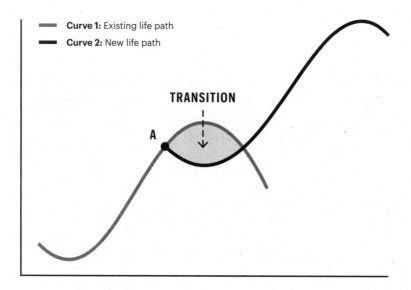

Consecutive S-curves

that randomness is not the determinant of the ultimate story. It's a bit player. Just a heckler in the audience of this complex, incredible production in which you own the next line. The next move. The next contribution.

Positive Chaos occurs in this beautiful space between what is now and what could be. It requires a leap of faith and new, transformed responses, which I am almost ready to impart to you. But first, we have just one more short chapter in Part One because there is a price to pay. The transfer from the curve you're on currently to the curve that will take you to the next level requires you first obtain a ticket. It won't cost you any money, but it may require you to let go of some cherished beliefs. Let's get crystal clear on the price of positive.

7

The Price of Positive

I F ANYONE could be understandably cynical, it's Ellen McCarthy. After serving in national intelligence agencies for three decades, on multiple boards, and teaching many classes in universities, she has seen a wide assortment of secret plots, disturbing trends, and negative information. Yet, she is entirely optimistic, hopeful, and positive: "I'm a dreamer. I believe that there is far more good than bad in the world. And there are many uncertain, negative things over-shadowing all the good that is out there. In so many ways, the world is the best it's ever been. This is where chaos is wonderful. You can make things better in big ways. You can set objectives, connect, and move people in positive directions. I'm actually a huge fan of chaos."

Ellen's newest endeavor, for which she is extremely passionate, is as the CEO of the nonprofit Truth in Media Cooperative. Its mission is to restore confidence in an industry that currently suffers quite negative public opinion and is lacking in public trust: news media. "We're bringing together news organizations across all types of media—from paper and print to broadcasting and social—that agree to come together and operate under specific tradecraft standards. The same standards we use in the intelligence community. We agree to abide by specific ethics, morals, and processes, and operate that way. We also work with educational institutions to incentivize students to think more critically."

Through Truth in Media, partnering outlets would become certi-fied (think Consumer Reports or the Good Housekeeping Institute) as organizations that are operating with the highest of integrity, presenting verified news with confirmed sourcing through ethical conduct. And if ever an industry needed an integrity overhaul, it is the news media. According to Gallup, in 2022, both print media and television media reached all-time lows in consumer confidence (an astonishing 16 percent and 11 percent, respectively).

Negative chaos is a drug. And like any addictive drug, giving in to it provides you with an escape mechanism from responsibil-ity, especially as extreme, unpredictable circumstances are out of your control. No matter where you look, you have a buffet of built-in excuses and justifications for mediocrity. It seems the entire world agrees and amplifies that our "new normal" is perpetual Challeng-ing, Hectic, Anxious, Overwhelming Stress. Get used to it, bucko. Share the sucky-ness, take a deep hit, then pass it around to the rest of us schlubs.

First, can we talk for a second about that term I just used? No, not *schlubs*. The term I'm referring to is *new normal*. I apologize for giving more airtime to what is, without a doubt, one of the most overused phrases of the early twenty-first century. Right up there with *unprecedented* and *pivot*. It's also, upon closer inspection, a ridiculous construct, and an instrument for managing expectations downward.

What is "normal" anyway? In my view, *normal* is a word we use to describe what used to be because we now more clearly understand the past. The challenges of today, however, always appear unique in some ways. They are, in the sense that they possess qualities and characteristics of now—the uncertainty and randomness of the moment. In another respect they are, upon closer examination, new versions of repeating patterns and similar circumstances that have happened in the world and in your life over the course of time. This fact is absolutely critical to recognize. Instead of looking at change as a deviation from the past, see it as a precedent for the future. How you handle what's in front of you creates more of that intention.

By now you understand that systems are complex and constantly changing. You also are aware we cannot go backward or undo anything (the irreversibility principle). Life only goes one way—forward.

Now Normal

Normalcy doesn't exist. All you ever get is *now*. Living doesn't happen in your past or future, but only in the moments as you experience them. If you want more peace, control, happiness, or success, or if you desire better health, results, opportunity, or impact, then your first commitment must be to embrace and leverage the now.

Do you really want your moments to be normal, predictable, ordinary, routine, or finite? Because, in truth, your unique *now* is extraordinary and infused with infinite possibilities. And if your now ever feels normal, then you may not be fully aware or engaged.

So rather than hoping to discover a new normal, how about choosing a *now normal*? Make a commitment, informed by your recent past, that you will fully engage your moments in intentional ways from now on.

1   **Pay attention.** Don't let the moments and opportunities slip by you.

2   **Give your all.** Don't hold back. Contribute useful ideas. Make "extra effort" your personal brand.

3   **Appreciate what is.** Rather than focusing on what is lacking in your life, default to appreciate your circumstances while they happen!

4   **Honor others.** Elevate those who share your moments and your life.

5   **Celebrate.** Laugh, smile, play, praise. Give thanks for this beautiful life and its unpredictable nature.

You can make this concept your own and adjust your normal "default settings" for how you engage with life. Demand more of yourself while capturing the magic and beauty around you.

That you picked up this book indicates you intuitively understand there exists greater meaning and accomplishment in the increasing chaos. And you are correct! That you've made it this far means you are both serious and curious. You are open to expanding your awareness and options beyond previous reactions and limitations. The chapters in Part Two will guide you through five specific transformations of your response system that will bring you a different "drug of choice." You'll attain the addictive ability to surf the waves of chaos with an entirely different perspective and a new set of skills. However, as you make the choice to engage in this process, you must be aware of the price.

Positivity's Price

In exchange for the transformation to Positive Chaos, there are a few things you'll need to give up. For many people the first of these may be too challenging and precious to part with.

Victimhood

Part of the seduction of negative chaos is that life is happening *to you*. You're simply *reacting* to the circumstances, rather than playing the leading role in *creating* them. I do not mean to diminish the importance of your past, or the significance of pain, loss, abuse, tragedy, indignation, bullying, or unfair treatment. However, I will tell you the pain of your past can be transformed into power in the present. Your suffering can be a healing process that bestows incredible empathy and a deep ability to help others.

You are absolutely entitled to your misery, limitations, and cynicism because of past events and circumstances or actions of others. But the entrenched position of justifiable hardship can be intoxicating and hard to transcend if you remain in that cycle of thinking. As you release some hardship, you may also find that some of your past identifications, limitations, and certainties loosen their hold on you. As that happens, it may be tempting to reach for them, as if to save an old friend from falling. Let them go. Embrace your emergence as a transformed individual.

Negative relationships

Do you have a friend who calls you just to complain? They're not seeking advice or guidance so much as acknowledgment and permission to feel miserable. The subtext to the conversation is, "I just need you to agree with me." Perhaps you do agree and find yourself wallowing in the friend's misery as well. This is when you know that negative chaos is likely present within that relationship.

The journey to attain the mindset and skill set of Positive Chaos is like reaching a higher orbit over your challenges. Once you begin to see better options, you will recognize the incredible waste of energy and effort required to maintain a lower orbit in life. You'll understand the limitations of negative thinking and no-win arguments. You'll also be able to recognize whether someone is truly willing to grow, or spectacularly pretending. You'll lose patience for indulging others' delusions or in having pointless interactions. Choosing to not participate or respond as expected will set you apart and may disrupt relationships, especially where codependency is involved.

Friends and loved ones who love to complain or express fear of impending disaster will find little interest in practices of Positive Chaos. However, others may be intrigued by your example, those who are open to a different perspective and a better way forward. For those individuals, you'll have the tools to offer genuine help, a valuable perspective, and mutual accountability.

Excuses

Excuses are defensive attempts to lessen blame, or to justify results and actions or a lack of action. If we are serious, and committed to an outcome or growth process, we look at what happened and own the results. We don't reprimand ourselves or others, nor do we wallow in self-pity. That helps nothing. We learn. We adjust. We recommit, or release the intention entirely, realizing that it's beyond the scope of what we previously envisioned. We understand that's an option, and we don't judge it as failure. We move on.

As you embrace Positive Chaos, you will lose interest in making excuses, blame becomes unimportant, and justification is simply a waste of time and energy. You take a more sober and straightforward approach to intention, action, and accountability.

Weak excuses such as "I didn't have time" become clear understandings like "this clearly wasn't a priority for me." Or "I underestimated what was required." By sidestepping the excuses, you also get to own the learning, and the honest assessment of what happened. You make corrections and become more careful in making commitments. You learn to say no, and to manage distractions differently. You become a person who is conscientious of time and known for following through on promises.

YOU WILL pay a price to transform yourself through Positive Chaos. It will separate you from some people. However, it will also bring you closer to others. You will surrender your excuses and step away from victimizing yourself. In exchange, you'll gain unprecedented traction toward whatever compelling ambitions you seek. You will also gain self-awareness and self-respect and fuel greater self-confidence. And, as you play the games of life and business at a new level, you'll achieve a profound curiosity and fascination for life's beauty and mystery.

So, are you okay with the price? Do you understand what's required and what's to be gained? All right, then. Let's keep going.

When you *react* to life, you perpetuate existing patterns and similar future scenarios. To *improve* your circumstances, you must *respond* differently than you have in the past. The next part of the book presents five specific transformations to help you stop reacting and start responding.

PART TWO

RESPOND

---

81 percent of working Americans think the future

will be shaped by how people *respond* to chaos.

Impact of Chaos in the American Workforce,
danthurmon.com/research

8

Transformation 1
Intentional Challenge

L IFE GLIMPSES moments of ease and bliss but exists in the constancy of struggle. When we exert mental and physical effort toward meaningful ends, we are truly alive.

Some people, like Tabassum Zalotrawala, global chief development officer of Chipotle Mexican Grill, are hardwired to turn chaos into advantage. "In the midst of crisis, all I see is opportunity," she told me. "In my world during the pandemic, this meant an opportunity to negotiate real estate agreements and proceed with confidence when others were hesitant. We also used social media to rapidly expand our platform to deliver great food to your home or make it available for safe pickup. This was not going to slow us down. We just needed to find new, and even better, ways of doing things."

However, for others, this ability to turn chaos into opportunity requires intentional strategies, like those you'll learn later in this chapter.

The first transformation isn't a change of condition, but an exchange of ownership. We're moving from just holding on, or simply reacting to "challenging times," to *intentionally challenging yourself*. In doing so, you will become the architect of your life and learning. You will acquire a new perspective on your hardships and problems. Instead of seeing them as rigid assignments or immovable obstacles, you will learn to see challenges as beneficial and shapable. You will also become more selective in the obligations you accept. This way, you set up situations and circumstances that are not a question of whether you win or lose. You win either way. Victory is assured before you even start.

---

69 percent of working Americans say they would be motivated to grow themselves if they personally chose to do so, versus being forced by someone else.

Impact of Chaos study

Time for a Test

What is the biggest challenge you're currently facing? Does the thought of it intimidate you and make you feel weak and tired? Perhaps there is so much at stake you don't know where to start or how you'll possibly get through it.

I've just characterized challenge from the perspective of negative chaos: Everything is hard. It's all too much. I will never be able to get through it. Even *if* I can, I don't really want to, and I can't imagine being satisfied by the results. Plus, right behind this challenge is another, even bigger one. They never end. Like the levels of a video game, the screen and scene quickly reload with another, more difficult mission.

I was ten years old in 1978 when my dad brought home the first computer I ever touched. This wasn't our computer, mind you. The concept of a personal computer didn't yet exist! This was a machine he was selling for work, the marvel of a new age, the promise of processing and productivity, and the dawn of video games. The green monochrome monitor and blinking cursor beckoned me. I learned elementary BASIC programming. We ran Will Crowther's groundbreaking program, *Adventure*, a text-based game in which you explored an unfamiliar cave system, acquiring tools and treasure.

My favorite program, however, was the classic *Space Invaders*, developed by Tomohiro Nishikado. This was a shooter game in which the player moved horizontally, taking cover behind rapidly disintegrating bunkers while firing at rows of alien ships dropping random bombs while descending upon you. Each level began with the aliens at the top of the screen, moving with the slow rhythm of an electronic, heart-beating soundtrack, reminiscent of the theme to the 1975 shark movie, *Jaws*. When the invaders reached the edge of the screen on either side, they moved closer, and the adrenaline-inducing music quickened. When you cleared a level, the next, more difficult one appeared. It all started over. It was so addictive, and never-ending. Well, that is, until you were killed by aliens. Three lives, and you're done.

Within a year, *Space Invaders* became a cabinet-based coin-operated video game. Other early favorites followed soon after: *Asteroids*, *Galaga*, *Defender*. Kids my age would travel to arcades and convenience stores with stacks of quarters to lose themselves (and their money) in fantasy.

This approach to addictive, perpetual combat resembles how most leaders approach challenges and how many people engage with life: Show up fresh, endure the onslaught. Fight, duck, and maneuver. Attain a fleeting victory, then start over again on more challenging levels until you ultimately lose. The biggest difference between a video game and reality, however, is you don't get three lives. You get one.

Allow me a quick philosophical pause to remind you that your life will one day cease to be. Although we cannot know how many, we all receive a finite number of days. We get one life, one chance to play in this realm of mystery and meaning. For a fleeting blip in the passage of time, we have a chance to learn and contribute ideas, experience wonder, build creations, and leave impressions upon people we will encounter. It seems to be human nature that we spend (or, from another perspective, waste) most of our days avoiding the undeniability of our mortality. Then, near the end of life, we suddenly see the big picture and understand both the magnitude and insignificance of the life we've experienced. (Unless you die suddenly, in which case it's over pretty quickly. Maybe that whole "life flashing before your eyes" thing happens. Not sure.)

The sooner you grasp the reality of your demise, the greater the appreciation and meaning you can bring to how you live. In doing so, you may change the way you choose to live today. Later in this book, I'll lead you through an exercise that will help you vividly imagine your funeral, which is more fun than you think.

But I Have To . . .

How many times in your life have you made the excuse that you don't have enough time? Or that you are unable to accept an invitation or opportunity because of a commitment or responsibility that is simply out of your control? It goes something like this:

I really would love to _____, but I *have to* _____.

Fill in the blanks. You have to work. You have to study. You have to care for someone else. You have to take on the tests and responsibilities thrust upon you. If you don't do it, nobody else will, so it's simply out of your control. You are the unfortunate casualty of previous commitments, a victim of your own productivity and responsible nature. You simply have to be there, do that, and spend your minutes, hours, and days—unrecoverable units of your lifetime—doing something you'd rather not, but have to, do.

Here is a shocking truth will rock your world: *you don't have to do anything.*

You don't have to go to work. You don't have to go to school, or study. You don't have to go see your parents, keep your promises to friends, prepare good meals, pay your bills and mortgage, save money for the future, or other myriad obligations you presume have been assigned to you.

Words matter immensely, and language is perhaps the most powerful and shapable real-time input of your life. The words you speak to yourself and to others will amplify in your thinking immediately, changing your relationship with your world. They also will change your external reality, future obligations, opportunities, self-discipline, and sense of well-being in enormous ways over time.

The words *have to* deprive you of power and choice, emphasizing external obligations and commitments. So, the first step to your first response transformation is to banish the phrase from your vocabulary entirely. This may sound innocuous, or even silly. Yet I promise, it will change your life.

Now, should you choose not to do some of those items previously mentioned, there will be consequences, such as losing your job and income, failing classes, defaulting on your debts, depriving yourself of loving relationships, betraying your principles, or forfeiting a reputation for responsibility. But because you are honest, smart, and forward-thinking, you choose to avoid those consequences. But when you claim you "have to" make a choice, you deprive yourself of the credit and self-discipline you deserve for having made the right choice.

You may also realize that there is plenty that you don't have to do, and probably shouldn't! When you question your obligations and assert your authority as decision-maker, you may suddenly see areas in your life where you are wasting your precious time and operating in ways that are incompatible with what you want and believe. That recognition places you in a powerful and unique position to dramatically shift your choices and behavior. However, that may create some disruption and chaos for those who have previously relied on you subordinating your decision-making authority. It may also create chaos for you that is short-term confusing and long-term astounding.

I Need To . . .

When you shift your language from the phrase *have to* to *need to*, you acknowledge you are making a choice. There is a purpose to my choice, which I recognize and claim. This gives you immediate power and clarity on what matters, and you get credit for that decision. Make this change today. Raise your awareness of the words you're using. Every time you use the phrase *have to*, replace it with *need to* until it becomes second nature.

I Get To...

The next stage in this process is to recognize that what you are choosing is not a "have to" obligation and is more than a "need to" choice. Your responsible decision is an incredible opportunity you "get to" accept. Not only that; you want it.

- I get to work, while others are struggling to find a job.

- I get to go to school and study, while others wish they had the opportunity.

- I get to demonstrate how much I love my parents, children, and friends because I have incredible people in my life.

- I get to pay my bills and mortgage while others can't afford to.

On the one hand, the phrase *get to* may come off a bit cheesy when spoken aloud. On the other hand, it certainly sets you apart, and will remind other people of their own good fortune. At the very least, using this phrase regularly can become an internal reminder for you that validates value, gratitude, and uniqueness: Not everyone experiences this, yet I do. This is something I can benefit from, learn from, or enjoy. These aren't obligations. They are gifts.

But changing your language isn't the only way you assert your ownership amid chaos. You also get to prescribe assignments and courses of learning for yourself.

Test Yourself

My friend Erik Weihenmayer was a freshman in high school when he started going blind. By the time he graduated, he had no sight whatsoever, but he still had an incredible internal vision of a path forward. Early on in his blindness, at fourteen years old, Erik heard about a class that was being offered, teaching rock climbing to kids. There was no explicit requirement for sight, so he decided to try it out and quickly discovered an obsession.

Erik found joy and purpose in the challenge of climbing rock walls, boulders, and eventually mountains, not by seeing a path forward, but by feeling it. He completely lost track of time immersed in the incredible test. He found his true nature, physical and mental strength, and self-confidence. Erik discovered he could climb using creativity and determination, and with the help of others to guide him. This combination of self will and dependence upon those he trusted made him feel anything but isolated. He was connected to people, to adventure, and to life. He had found his calling.

Erik Weihenmayer went on to become the first blind climber to summit Mount Everest and the rest of the Seven Summits (the highest peaks on all continents). He has also, perhaps even more impressively, kayaked the entire length of the Colorado River through the Grand Canyon. This unprecedented accomplishment, from inception to completion, is conveyed in Erik's riveting book *No Barriers*.

Erik is one of my favorite speakers on the planet because he is as precise with his use of language as he is with the placement of his hands and feet while ascending a rockface. We have climbed together on multiple occasions, including in Hong Kong, and I even taught Erik to juggle (sort of). He was my first and only blind student, and I found it fascinating to figure out how to convey the concepts and skills of a visual discipline to someone who cannot see. Although Erik will never be a juggling master, he did successfully complete a pattern of catches with three balls and both hands.

Today Erik leads groups of challenged individuals on adventurous expeditions. Whether they are wounded veterans, amputees, sight-challenged, or emotional scarred by PTSD, people learn to not let their barriers define them or prevent them from taking on a new adventure or a new test. I can personally attest that these adventures are life changing for all who participate.

WHEN UNCERTAINTY and randomness strike, whether the immediate perception is threatening or exciting, you don't take it personally. You simply see it as a new factor to incorporate into your life. The irreversibility principle (Chapter 4) liberates you from wasting valuable time and energy bemoaning what happened (and now cannot un-happen) and helps you shape what's happening now. What's happening next.

This is not about the challenge coming at you. It's about the challenge coming from you. It's not what's testing you, but how you are choosing to test yourself.

I've already discussed the professional response my team and I took when confronted with the realities of the COVID pandemic. While some people were jumping to the forefront to proclaim what they thought would happen or wasting enormous energy, effort, and time trying to guess how it would all play out, my team and I quickly recognized that most of that story was unknowable. That meant that projecting a best guess on the ultimate outcome or projecting fear and blame were equally useless strategies. Instead, we asked, "How will we grow through this? How are we choosing to test ourselves to get better and develop new professional capabilities?"

That questioning resulted in the team creating a digital broadcasting studio with multiple sets and cameras. We deepened our body of content, learned how to produce live "virtual" events that were remarkably more effective than what was standard, essentially leapfrogging over our competition in many ways. More importantly, we were helping people and companies that desperately needed help when they were most confused and vulnerable. And we were doing so by embodying the same principles we were teaching.

What's important to remember about that story is that it wasn't motivated by a master plan. There was no guarantee of success. We were as swept up in the pandemic chaos as anyone else. Yet we were motivated by the intentional challenge of it as well. What was your COVID breakthrough? What new skill or capability were you able to accelerate and attain because you needed to?

Since then we have heard many different versions of similar stories about how the enormity of the COVID challenge and (this is key) the interruption of existing patterns enabled people to elevate skills, accelerate growth and technology, and serve others in new ways. Of course, the hardships, fear, and loss were also present and significant. But it wasn't the only story. Positive Chaos and negative chaos coexist. Pick the polarity that serves you.

Life is rich with examples of people and teams who, when faced with adversity, found advantage. Every uncertainty contains some opportunity. Every downside has an upside. (Also, by the way, every upside has a downside. Please remember this when you fixate upon "up" in the excitement of incredible promise.)

Surrender to Victory

When you choose to test yourself during chaos, you are effectively saying, "Sure, I see that challenge. We're all dealing with that challenge. And also, while that whole mess is working itself out, which will take some time and is largely out of my control, I'm also choosing to test myself by learning and doing *this*."

Adopting intentional challenge is both a reclamation of power and an act of surrender. You are asserting your authority to climb a path of your choosing, and there is zero guarantee you'll get there. Just because you want to doesn't mean you can.

Yet here's the thing. When you choose to test yourself, you win either way. Because you took control and set yourself an intentional challenge and a course of learning, you will achieve victory in one of two ways.

1   You will attain what you sought to accomplish. Or...

2   You will learn something truly valuable about yourself and your circumstances.

Remember, life is defined by struggle. And it is precisely the hard stuff that reveals who we are and what we stand for. By choosing your struggle and staying the course, you are sculpting your story and your character, intentionally. This is largely internal work, as you spend the totality of your days in the confines of your thinking. Nobody else knows your struggles and victories like you do. The byproduct of all your internal effort, however, is an external example of a person who lived life truthfully, boldly, and bravely. You will be imperfect, fail, and fall short in many respects. You'll make mistakes, miss opportunities, and betray your own sacred principles. Then, you'll recover. Learn. Try again. Resolve what went wrong. Apologize where you caused harm. Continue climbing, ever more enabled by your honest, intentional struggle.

When you're experiencing chaos, it's difficult to avoid being swept up in the circumstances of the moment. It all seems so urgent, original, and demanding. Regardless of what came before, you may think the circumstances require an entirely new plan and new principles, right? Most likely, no.

Remember, life presents recurring patterns. Today's chaos is a new version of what you've already been through (more on that later). The key to working with chaos is your perspective. I challenge you to place more emphasis on the long-term recurring challenge versus the next right move. Bring the best of your current ability and commit to improvement. You don't have to understand the eventual payoff. In fact, you can't entirely. The reality that all you go through and overcome *does serve you* will be revealed in time.

Everything Counts

I paid my way through college, earning a business degree while building my own entertainment business. At first, this was mostly by delivering my one-man show as a comedy juggler and acrobat, or by performing my various skills at events, parties, and festivals. It was fun, challenging work, imbued with constant variety.

Every gig required navigating (sans GPS) to a location, often to one I had never been before. Based on both the previous requests from my clients and the real-time situation, which I could only know once I arrived (the performance space, audience, music, sound system, weather), I would draw from my previous experience and skill sets to deliver my best performance on the fly. I was good at this and quickly earned a reputation among meeting planners and entertainment agents as someone who always arrived early and did whatever it took to make the event a success. Of course, that ensured the requests for my services kept coming.

From the mid-1980s through 1994 I did hundreds of events and eventually produced bigger projects involving dozens of performers and greater complexity. From the extravagant to the absurd, these experiences ran the gamut. Each time I arrived at a new, uncertain test I would think, "I've never done this before! But what have I already done that is similar in some ways?" Asking that question, then finding an answer, no matter how remote, gave me confidence even though I was making it up as I went.

Early on in that journey, I had the unique opportunity to work for a man named Charlie. Charlie was a promoter in rural North Georgia who fancied himself a modern-day P.T. Barnum. He put on shows by the name "Children's Magical Circus" in school gymnasiums. His methods were questionable, but his motives were pure. Well, mostly.

Charlie would give away free tickets to children in their classrooms and encourage them to bring their whole family to this amazing event. On the day of the performance, parents would discover the fine print that the free tickets were only good for kids under a certain age. Parents and older siblings had to buy their own tickets, which, of course, once they were there (with excited children in tow), they felt obligated to do.

Charlie also sold popcorn, drinks, and balloons on sticks (he didn't have a helium tank). The circus had only four performers: my friend Doug McCart, a magician; Doug's wife, Greta, a ventriloquist; a fire eater named Jerry, who was in his sixties; and me. Charlie loved to work with me because I brought the backdrop, sound system, and at least three distinct acts to round out the show. Charlie moved around a lot, sleeping mostly at economy motels, and there was no way you could reach him. He called you from a payphone to arrange the date, and always paid in cash—sometimes in change. I always got my money, but Doug wasn't quite so lucky.

The whole undertaking was bizarre. Charlie suffered from halitosis and didn't keep the best personal hygiene. Our encounters always left me with a lingering, sensory-rich memory. I'd often find myself driving the two hours back to college (and my 7:50 a.m. class) thinking, "What just happened?" However, we were bringing live entertainment to communities that wouldn't have had it otherwise. I always delivered my best and gave them something special to share and remember. Families left laughing and smiling as they returned to their lives with new memories, holding sticks with balloons tied on top.

Since those days, my life and professional work have changed remarkably. In addition to entertainment, I bring messages and solutions. I've spoken to thousands of audiences on six continents, including top leaders of the most respected companies on the planet. I've delivered the closing keynote for the Million Dollar Round Table before an international audience of eight thousand while simultaneously being translated into a dozen languages. I was inducted into the Speaker Hall of Fame and have served as president of the National Speakers Association. And on some level, as I step into those experiences and even greater opportunities that await me, I know that I have a claim to confidence that can be traced back to experiences that include those shows for Charlie. The tenacity, variety, creativity, and sheer repetition of my past prepared me, every step of the way, for the next level. I wouldn't trade a moment of it.

All that you've experienced—the good and the bad (and the weird)—is part of your learning journey. Your past has shaped your skills and character, taught you resolve and resilience. Your successes have given you confidence and validation. Glimpses of greatness. And your failures have provided humility and valuable evidence that, yes, you can survive the tough stuff. What's more, your personal repertoire of life experience is uniquely yours and extraordinarily valuable. Nobody else has your exact story.

Everything counts, but you don't have to count it. It all serves you, but you don't need to know exactly how.

Ask Better Questions

When you perceive challenges as external, or coming at you, you are operating in survival mode. In that mindset, you will ask low-level questions that keep you in the mode of survival and scarcity. Questions such as these:

- Why is this happening to me?

- How will we get through this?

- How long will this last? When will it ever end?

- What do I have to do right now?

- How do I stay safe and protect myself and those I love?

- How can I understand everything when it's all too much?!

You might make a case for why these questions are important, especially when it comes to discerning the next move or ensuring safety and protection. Agreed! The problem is your brain doesn't draw a distinction between actual physical threat and simple confusion resulting from newness or complexity. To your limbic system—the part of the brain concerned especially with emotion and survival behavior—a threat to your current sense of self or your present perspective is similar to a threat to your survival. Both sets of challenges can cause intense emotional repercussions, including elevated heart rate and fear. In this state, you are more inclined to evade than to create. You're more equipped to flee than to grow. You're more likely to protect the precarious state of what was than to innovate what is next.

One of the most effective ways to shift from the "survival challenge" mindset to the "intentional challenge" mindset is to start asking better questions. What follow are three of my favorites, which will help elicit the challenge coming *from you*.

Question one: What are you working on and excited about? This question changes the focus from trying to discern what's happening (life happening to you) and presumes some initiative and desire. What's your intentional challenge? What are you working on or working toward? What are you excited about? What are you trying to make happen in the world?

Question two: What does this require you to learn? Again, we are making a positive presumption. You are learning, and that's a good thing. It's not about what you're dealing with or what you must do to survive. The even more empowering question is: What does your current intentional challenge require you learn? To answer this question, you must claim your learning. Yeah, I've been learning a lot, and I'm going to learn even more!

Question three: Who are you becoming in the process? With this question you're asking yourself or someone else, "How will you be different as you complete this undertaking you're working on and the learning you're experiencing? How is it changing you?" Although this may seem a little esoteric, this question will illuminate the truth of the human journey. We're not just doing stuff, or simply surviving. We're constantly in the process of *becoming*.

Incidentally, these questions are also tremendous ways to get into meaningful conversations with people you encounter, work with, or love. Asking a question such as "How are you growing?" or "Who are you becoming?" reveals genuine interest and a positive expectation for others. Essentially, you are saying, "We're all learning and growing together. What can I learn from you?"

In my work with leaders and their teams, I incorporate these three questions within a broader culture of learning. Anyone with an organization can ask these questions at any time of anyone else— from the CEO to the frontline workers. We should all know our own answers.

So, what are you working on and excited about? What is that requiring you to learn? And who are you becoming in the process?

If you have a glimpse of those answers, please capture them now! And if not, don't worry. That's what the rest of the book is all about, and I'll guide you through the process.

As you practice the shift from dealing with challenges to asserting intentional and self-directed challenges through the methods I've shared with you, you will experience improved control and ownership of life. Chaos won't throw you as easily. Instead, it will inspire you to act! Now, let's move to the second transformation to provide you greater mastery of your personal pace and well-being.

SKILLSET EXERCISE
INTENTIONAL CHALLENGE

1 **Watch your language.** Closely scrutinize the words you think and use in your internal dialogue. Understand that every sentence and sentiment uttered or internalized either empowers negative chaos or emboldens your intentional positive pursuits. Consistently select better words and more empowering language.

2 **Take on a no-lose challenge.** Test yourself with a new skill or course of learning that will undoubtedly stretch you, regardless of how it turns out.

3 **Release what you cannot control.** Obsessing over what is outside your control is a de facto choice *not* to handle or improve what is.

9

Transformation 2
From Hectic to Healthy

ONICA ROTHGERY started her career with Yum! Brands in 1992 as a restaurant manager for Taco Bell. When she was a second lieutenant in the US Army, Monica cultivated personal discipline and gained valuable experience leading teams. So, it wasn't long before she advanced through the organization, attaining leadership positions with Pizza Hut, then KFC, where, at the time of this writing, she serves as the chief operations officer (COO) for more than 4,100 restaurants in America.

In a recent interview, Monica gave me an interesting twist on the effects of the COVID pandemic on her life and work:

> Everyone acted like the pandemic was the crisis, and in many ways it was. Many people lost lives, or family members. On a personal level, it was devastating. But on a business level, in my business and among my peers, the crisis is *now*. Businesses can't get supplies as the supply chain is a mess. The wait time on equipment and parts is up to a year. The labor force didn't return, and so we don't have enough people to run our restaurants. These are challenges unlike anything we've seen in forty years. People are polarized and exhausted. With leadership, you have to be upbeat, resourceful, and more creative than ever.

Considering these chaotic challenges, daily emergencies, weather events, supply chain issues, and the complexity of running a fifty-person operations team that supports over four thousand KFC restaurants, Monica operates in an environment that is certainly hectic. So, I asked her how effective she is at prioritizing her health. "Self-care is really important to me, Dan. It has to be at the top of my list. I have a fitness and nutrition coach. I'm always tuned in to the business, and I have a great team that supports me. But the end of the day, I can quiet my mind at least 70 to 80 percent. I go to bed at nine o'clock and sleep for eight hours."

Consider, for a moment, Monica's insights and example as a leader in her organization. In the midst of what is unquestionably a hectic, stressful, daily challenge that impacts the lives of thousands of restaurant owners and tens of thousands of employees, Monica recognizes she cannot adequately serve others unless she first shows up for herself and can shut down to rest and recharge. As a result, she stays fit, and she looks and feels far younger than her years, despite the demands of life and business.

DO YOU find yourself moving at a frantic pace, struggling to keep up with all that is happening? Is that approach, which seems unavoidable, taking a toll on the state of your health? If so, you're not alone. Consider this statistic.

More than half of working Americans experience multiple negative health effects (mental distress, less sleep, poor eating habits, lack of exercise) regularly due to the pace of their lives.

Impact of Chaos study

The second transformation of Positive Chaos is to recalibrate your internal sense of time while improving your physical and mental health. You can't outrun change, but you can better manage your energy, put forth effective effort, and find a sense of calm within calamity. You can move from always feeling behind to setting your schedule, and from feeling perpetually worn out to a more consistent feeling of well-being. You can thrive at the speed of life.

Few people will argue that the pace of life and speed of change have increased dramatically during our lifetime. We can access information anywhere, at the touch of a screen. Pulling out a phone has become a reflex, often preempting our own thinking, problem-solving, or creative reasoning. Boredom is banished, and we seek to fill every space of available time with a distraction such as a "productive" activity (like deleting unwanted emails); communicating via text, DM, Snap, call, or FaceTime (as we're always available for interruptions); escaping into social media feeds; or playing our current favorite addictive game.

The question today for me and you is, what is and what isn't productive, meaningful, and useful? A large portion of what you lump into life's busyness is not truly helpful. Yet even if you can steer clear of self-distraction, perhaps you might presume that an effective life must feel frenetic and requires you to accelerate to the point of near-breaking.

Here's the problem. If your primary move is to race life, life has no problem speeding up with you. And, as life never tires or wears out (and—spoiler alert—you do!), you will eventually lose that race. Hectic isn't healthy in the long term. It's not sustainable. And it certainly doesn't equate to happiness.

Hectic to Healthy

The connection between a hectic mode of operation and compromised health may at first seem erroneous. Isn't it possible to be healthy and fit and live at a frenzied pace? Absolutely. In fact, those who are fit clearly have internal drive, which they can deploy abundantly. I want you to have great physical and mental health while living a full and productive life, at whatever pace you choose.

However, according to our research, that simply isn't the case for the vast majority of people. Feeling behind or operating with hectic tendencies is a nearly universal experience that carries consequences.

Worry and mental distress top the list of negative health effects from hectic living (54 percent of participants experience this daily).

Impact of Chaos study

We also discovered interesting distinctions between groups of participants in the study. For instance, women are 7.8 percent more likely than men to experience *all* the negative health effects we tested due to the pace of their lives. Gen Z participants (eighteen to twenty-six years old) are significantly more likely than other generations to experience poor eating habits. And older millennials (thirty-six to forty-five years old) are significantly more likely to experience a lack of exercise and less sleep.

Many people assume and act as though some detrimental impact to their health is simply the necessary, unavoidable cost of success or modern life. Maintaining their commitments, advancing goals, and sustaining mental and physical health seem (to most) to be mutually exclusive propositions. But it doesn't have to be that way.

I want you to have sustainable productivity *and* a healthier way of being. Hectic doesn't work in the long run. It isn't very useful in the short run either. When operating in "hectic mode" you make yourself upset, nervous, and agitated. This also agitates the people around you. You make mistakes more easily and overlook important details. The internal condition of "hectic-ness" creates internal conflict and disrupts feelings of calm or contentment.

The word *disease*, when broken into its component parts, *dis-ease*, literally means "lack of ease." You can make yourself and those around you sick, creating mental and physical illness, because of how you think and engage in your life. It's harder to think useful thoughts or follow through on positive agendas (including maintaining your health) when you operate in a hectic state. If you're a leader of a company, a team, or a family, hectic energy doesn't promote confidence and loyalty. In fact, it has the opposite effect.

To help you make this critical transformation from hectic to healthy, the rest of this chapter will provide perspective on your sense of urgency and teach you how to set a more deliberate pace, attain new mental strategies, and adopt a more sustainable approach to mental and physical well-being. Positive Chaos can lead to greater mental and physical health, even in the midst of the madness.

I Need It NOW!

Urgency is a huge contributor to hectic-ness and the experience of negative chaos. This takes the form of demands placed on you by others or yourself that constitute intense time-sensitive matters. "This *must* happen *today*." Or "I *need* an answer *immediately*." Often this is an item someone should have foreseen earlier, but that they just thought of at the last minute.

There's a certain thrill that comes from handling the urgent, like playing Whac-A-Mole with life's emergencies. But is this the best way to spend your time and effort? Is it healthy and sustainable? Efficient and productive? What is your intentional response when urgency is presented to you? And here's the big question: *Is your current default response to urgency reducing future urgencies, or is it promoting behavioral patterns that will deliver more of the same?*

Years ago, when we were producing large scale events, we were regularly bombarded with last-minute, panic-induced, urgent requests, such as a complex proposal that was needed immediately. In such instances we developed a go-to response: "Lack of preparation on your part does not constitute an emergency on our part." Granted, this is not something we generally said to our customers. It's more of an internal mantra, or something we said to each other. It's a reminder that we have a choice about how we engage in the situation. The idea that we must scramble to deal with something because it was framed as an emergency is one we don't have to accept. We always have a choice.

When presented urgent decisions regarding investment opportunities or other important matters, my response is to slow it down. This isn't something that came naturally, but I cultivated this after realizing through experience that "today only" opportunities don't generally play out well. When placed in a state of urgency, I don't think as clearly or consider all the facts. So, when others push me to go faster, I usually respond by deliberately slowing down.

Finding Space in the Pace

Our son is a skilled guitarist. To be more exact, Eddie's a "shredder," which means that he not only plays well, he also plays fast. Having practiced and studied the instrument for the most of his life, including at the esteemed Berklee College of Music in Boston, Eddie is proficient in many styles and genres, including jazz, pop, rock, and classical. He deeply understands music theory. He loves it all, yet is most inclined to play metal, where the pace and complexity of the musical melodies are pushed to the limits of human ability. He loves the test of truly difficult pieces that take time to master. To perform such challenging works requires diligent practice, muscle memory, and both mental and physical dexterity. What's interesting is that mastery is measured not just in playing the notes, but in playing them cleanly, with distinct space between them, even at feverish speeds.

Music happens in the space between the notes. Otherwise, it's all just a blur of noise. I asked Eddie recently, "How is that possible? How exactly did you develop the ability to play so fast?" His answer: "You play slow, perfectly."

In a similar way, juggling five objects at once (something I practice daily) can appear chaotic, yet it is an act that's incredibly organized and deliberately paced. The objects travel in a recurring pattern (system), looping from one hand toward a target above the opposite hand. Once it reaches its peak, the object descends to be caught and is relaunched into another symmetrical throw toward a target above the opposite hand. This pattern takes the shape of an infinite loop resembling the wings of a butterfly. I find it fascinating that this form, which I've honed since I was eleven years old, is also the foundation of the Lorenz attractor.

Juggling has been the metaphor at the core of my philosophy and professional work for three decades. Clearly, it is representative of the challenges we face in life and work: managing multiple objects (or objectives) with skill and effectiveness. Taken in total, our lives seem overwhelming, but in truth we are managing one "throw" at a time. Juggling is a fantastic illustration, as it allows people to learn visually, understand the concept of patterns, and see the distinct difference between an approach that is hectic or rushed versus a pattern with the same number of objects approached with a sense of relaxation.

You can't handle everything at once. You handle the throw in your hand with excellence and precision. While it's out of your hands, it's also out of your control. You must let it go, realizing your ability to influence its flight has ended. You're aware of it, because of your perspective and understanding of the pattern. You know you'll get another chance to catch and redirect it, yet your primary attention is on the next throw—the one leaving your hand at this moment.

When I say "spaces between" the notes, or throws and catches, please understand that what I'm really talking about is the spaces between your thoughts and actions. Between what you were doing, and what you're doing next. What you hear, and how you choose to respond. What surprises you, and your initial reaction. These *moments between* represent the *phase space* in which your personal experience of chaos transpires. This is where you create and contribute your inputs, whether they are reflexive and automatic, or intentional and deliberately different than what you might have done in the past.

To move from hectic to healthy, you must learn to expand and use the moments between stimulus and response. And although you measure your life in days, months, years, and decades, all you ever get are the *moments*. Who you are today and what you've achieved—your profession, relationships, health, and quality of life—are the products of your inputs to moments of your past.

How have you done? Are you pleased with your results to date? What have you attained and become thus far?

Whether you are satisfied or humbled, the best response is to elevate inputs going forward. Recommit to doing better at experiencing and using your moments. This self-prescribed course of study, your intentional test, includes learning to better manage your focus and attention while developing better disciplines and responses. And every day provides ample opportunity to practice.

Redefining Work

Many people use urgency and time scarcity as excuses for lacking performance, inadequate participation, or half efforts. Having too much to do and not enough time to do it absolves one of responsibility and helps justify poor results. Intentions should suffice, we rationalize. If only we weren't so busy, we would be more productive. There's just too much "work" to do.

We all get the same amount of time. You get all there is, every day, for the entirety of your lifetime. It is a universal commodity apportioned equally to all. Granted, some people have existing obligations that demand more of their time. Certain jobs and educations require more time to accomplish, leaving less to distribute as desired. I get it. Your current time obligations and entanglements are a result of previous commitments and choices—patterns of your past. To reset and recalibrate your relationship with the clock takes (pun intended) *time*.

However, what is also true is that this transformation and complete shift of mindset could happen in a single moment. It takes intentional choices now and increased presence and responsibility. Perhaps a good place to start is a new definition of *work*:

work (verb)

To be actively engaged in thought and activity that truly matters.

Go with me on this. What if your job isn't just your job? Your job is to live an honest, healthy, and meaningful life. You get one chance to do this well; to exist and contribute on this planet. You started wherever you started. You made choices that created some paths of possibility and eliminated others. Much of what transpired is irreversible. Yet even now, infinite possibilities exist before you. Looking back from the eventual certainty of your demise, whether a week away or many decades, you'll have crystal clarity about what truly mattered. What if you could capture more of that understanding today and use it as your lens for discernment and measure of progress?

From this perspective, you are at work from the minute you're awake, striving to understand and engage in what matters, relative to your moments and circumstances. Your work involves how you treat other people, how you treat yourself, what you say and do in all situations, and how you strive to develop and live chosen principles.

When actively engaged in your profession, you'll develop an intolerance to be at work and not working! When you're showing up, but not contributing, you're wasting time (yours and your employer's), taking up space, and missing the greatest gift of a job that goes far beyond a paycheck—personal pride and satisfaction in doing what matters to the best of your ability. Make this your standard, and you may realize you're in the wrong job. Or perhaps you're in the perfect job with the wrong mindset. You'll begin to see opportunities to take initiative, even though it may be outside your job assignment. Complete departures from your daily agenda may prove to be the most valuable contribution you can deliver. That's Positive Chaos at work.

I can hear you already: "Dan, that sounds wonderful and all. It's also unrealistic. My boss requires me to follow protocols, and demands that I do it their way." Maybe that's true. Maybe it's not as true as you think. Perhaps you can demonstrate a better way to drive results and make an impact through your insights and example. And just maybe this initiative and courage you demonstrate is the Positive Chaos that instigates your advancement and leadership ability. Or maybe it leads you down a path to an entirely different revelation about who you are and how you can best contribute and create in the world.

I recognize what I'm describing here is a type of drive and commitment that seems rare these days. The opportunity here, though, is that it's never been easier to distinguish yourself by setting a positive example!

Currently, we are facing a crisis of willingness to work. The biggest issue and major concern of nearly every one of my clients is the same, regardless of the industry. You guessed it: Labor. Workforce. People. Either they can't find qualified, reliable people, they can't keep them, or they can't motivate the people they have to do what they were hired for. Certainly nothing more than that. People just don't seem to care as much. Loyalty appears to have flown out the window, and job-hopping for bigger checks or signing bonuses is common practice.

There is no single solution to these complex challenges, but there are approaches that are far more effective in attracting and incentivizing qualified, capable human beings. I will go deeper into these ideas and strategies in our chapter on leading through chaos. For now, however, it's important to recognize two truths:

1 The era of viewing a worker without consideration for that person's well-being is over. If your job isn't a net plus to someone's life, their willingness becomes extremely limited, and they won't likely be with you for long.

2 After experiencing COVID, the equation for what constitutes a good or great employment opportunity has changed entirely. I'll break this truth down for you in Chapter 16.

Managing Deliberate Attention

By now you understand you are not a victim of your hectic life. You have all the time there is and the agency to choose how you use and experience it. You can expand moments with intention, make new choices, and take different actions than you have in the past. Even if you aren't fully convinced, hopefully, I have your attention. Because *deliberate attention* is exactly what you must master to transform hectic to healthy and to orchestrate Positive Chaos.

Placing your focus

In my speeches, I often use audience participation to create more lasting lessons by teaching through engaging experiences. For example, I use peacock feathers to teach concepts related to balance, including the importance of placing focus. First, I have audience members look at their hands while attempting to balance the feathers, which proves frustrating and ineffective. Next, I ask them to shift their attention to the top of the feather, and instantly the challenge becomes easy. Nearly effortless. With the proper perspective, the "right moves" become intuitive. Try this yourself with any long, lightweight object, and notice how by focusing on the top of the object, you can anticipate what is necessary.

The lesson in this first feather exercise is that focusing on principles, goals, and values is so important. When you place your attention upon what matters, you simplify hectic distractions, reduce complexity, and perform with greater confidence and competence.

The next feather challenge is trickier: I ask the audience to balance the feather, then throw it into the air, catching it in the other hand and resuming a new balance. This now involves not just one point of focus, but an active strategy of managing attention. First, you are looking at the top of the feather, as before. Easy. Then you push the feather straight up, with force, sending it flying vertically into the air. Now, your attention must quickly shift from the top of the feather to the other end, the pointed tip, which you hope to catch in your other hand. Then, immediately after you see it, and as you're on your way to make the catch, you shift your attention right back to the top of the feather, to resume the balance, this time with your other hand.

Once I present the challenge, pandemonium ensues. Feathers are flying. People are frantically trying what I've described, and the initial approach is one of hectic acceleration. Assuming they must go super-fast to make this work, they race their minds and hands to pull it off. They also talk a lot, which is interesting. For an exercise in which I've given complete instructions, none of which involves speaking, the chatter in the room immediately amplifies.

I let this go on for about thirty seconds, then I inject some calm clarity by demonstrating what I've described happens far more slowly than they think. By pushing the peacock feather a bit higher into the air, effectively increasing the "space between," you have plenty of time to place your focus exactly where you want it to be in a manner that is unhurried and effective. Look at the top, then the tip, then back to the top. Remember to breathe. At this point, the break-throughs start to happen, and soon we have a room full of calm and confident feather balancing masters.

Then, I debrief the lesson to ensure it is forever linked to the fun, shared experience: In life you are constantly encountering attractors of your attention. When you can resist the attractors and instead place your focus where you want it to be, you can approach what is hectic in a more healthy and effective way.

Strengthening your attention muscle

We live in a world where your attention is constantly being demanded. The masters of misdirection—marketers, headline writers, complainers, and other attention seekers—employ technology, creativity, and relentless persistence to interrupt your next purposeful thought. Even while writing this on my laptop, news alerts and text messages pop up in the corner of my screen, beckoning me away from you. I find myself thinking, "I thought I turned those off. Did they turn themselves back on again with the latest update?"

Many people and powerful organizations don't want you to stay focused. They want your focus *on them*. They have studied exactly how to separate you from your intentional mind, how to pull you into their world of distraction and previously scheduled programming. Speed is their friend, the elusive notion that their message is urgently important, and the implication that if you just race a bit faster, assuming a more hectic pace, you'll be able to absorb or do their thing, then get back to yours eventually.

Managing your attention is the art of placing your focus where you want it to be. This is not only more enjoyable, but also far more effective for getting things done during changing circumstances. When it comes to mental health, this skill of managing attention and presence is also the essence of *mindfulness*. Often, this is practiced through meditation, breathing exercises, and guided experiences. It can also be experienced right now and throughout your life by bringing your full attention deeply into the present moment. Observe details you otherwise would have missed. Choose to draw your attention to something different than what others are seeing, and immediately you will have asserted and strengthened your "attention muscle."

Meditation sounds mysterious, but it is quite simple. With eyes closed, for a designated time (usually around twenty minutes, but you can start with ten), you sit quietly. The objective is to quiet the mind, but it isn't necessary to think of nothing. That's a common misunderstanding, that you should figure out how to clear your mind of all thoughts. That's ridiculous. Have you looked in there lately? Your mind is incredibly overcrowded. It's like a hoarder's attic! Stuff you're trying to remember, and memories you can't seem to forget. Thoughts and projects stacked upon other thoughts and projects, going way back to the beginning of your consciousness. There's a lot of old junk you just can't seem to get rid of. You thought you gave that away but it's still here, gathering dust in the corner.

Meditation involves placing your consciousness on an intentional point of focus, usually your breathing, a mantra, or awareness of a specific detail. You could focus on a place in your body, a particular sound, or even a movement. That's right, meditations can happen while you're moving, eyes open, out and about in the world. The key is to actively focus on one single thing. As you do, you are asserting your authority over your awareness. My mind is here. Now.

What happens next, predictably, is that your mind challenges that authority, like a rebellious child, by presenting you a distracting thought. That is totally normal. *What you do next is the essence of meditation.* Rather than become upset that your meditation was interrupted by a rude thought, you simply notice it, then let it go, bringing your focus back where you wanted it to be. That, right there, is what I think of as a "meditation rep." That's one. (Don't actually count your distractions, though. That can get very distracting.)

Meditation experts may balk at this simplification, but I find it extremely helpful. Every time you have a thought and choose not to indulge it, you strengthen your attention muscle and reassert your authority over your awareness. Effectively you're saying, "I see you there, distraction. Thank you for trying to help me, but now is not the time." Then, over time, these thoughts and distractions become quieter and less frequent.

Occasionally, you may experience periods of "no mind," that is, you gain freedom from both your thoughts and your intentional focus. But even those moments are fleeting. Every meditation is different. Just like going to the gym. Whether it's the best workout of your life or you struggle to accomplish even the basic routines, it still counts. You can't get fit in one workout. You can't become mindful in one sitting. Take your practice wherever you go.

Seizing the moment

Healthy productivity isn't just a matter of squeezing hours. It's about seizing moments. Inspiration (and even transformation) can happen in a blink. Often, opportunities are presented to you with little notice or advanced announcement. You cross paths with the right person, see someone in distress, or suddenly understand with clarity what you must say or do. It's in those moments we've been given glimpses of what's possible, and tests of our true intentions. When presented the chance or circumstance you desire or truly need, will you take it?

The problem is those moments are unpredictable and random. Such moments are the absolute essence of chaos: The intersection of determined effort (what you actively pursue) and what is uncertain and random. They don't usually happen without clarity of purpose and an investment of time previously dedicated to the advancement of a goal or meaningful learning. You show up for your life, put in the work, and demonstrate your commitment to learn and grow. Then, opportunities to learn and grow "show up" for you, like on-ramps to a highway for faster travel. Either you take the on-ramp, or you pass it by, in which case you'll likely travel a few more miles and encounter more pit stops and detours before the next on-ramp appears.

Warping time

I am blessed to be busy and to travel to a variety of interesting places. On rare occasions I can extend my trip a day or two and bring a family member with me. More often, I'm in a hurry to get home or continue onward to the next engagement. In these instances, I've honed the intention and skill of "warping time." Don't miss the moments you are given in the blur of what is "pressing" or "normal." Warp time and create space for the extraordinary. Time warping is an act of Positive Chaos. It's about saying, "Even though it makes sense to go this way, I'm choosing to go that way and create an experience." Let me offer an example.

I was speaking in Hong Kong for the first time ever and had decided to stay an extra two days before coming home. Then a client asked me if I would be interested in delivering a thirty-minute presentation at their event in Mauritius while I was "in the neighborhood." Now, looking at a map, this looks easily doable, but it involved flying fifteen hours each way to reach the island country east of southernmost Africa, just on the other side of Madagascar. My flights for Hong Kong were already purchased and nonrefundable. This Mauritius excursion would just barely fit into my Hong Kong window. Yet, not only did I want to do it, but it seemed like the necessary completion of an assignment I received decades prior.

As a high school junior, I was invited to participate in the Model United Nations (Model UN). This experience is a simulation of the United Nations General Assembly in which students become ambassadors to gather and discuss important issues and international relationships. My teacher had selected me to join a small group from our school to represent randomly assigned countries. I was designated the ambassador of the beautiful island country of, you guessed it, Mauritius. As the diplomat, I learned all about the country's beautiful island beaches on the Indian Ocean, its rainforests, hiking trails, and population of just over a million people. I knew about its desires to diversify its economy from primarily sugar production to include a variety of agriculture products, manufactured exports, financial services, and tourism. How could I say no to the opportunity to go see my beloved country?

After the fifteen-hour flight from Hong Kong, I had just a few hours left of daylight. That evening I'd attend my client's reception, then I'd get a good night's rest, speak the next morning, and fly back to Hong Kong. Yes, it's a quick trip, but such is the life of an ambassador. Always on the go! The question was what would I do with my precious few hours? How would I warp the little time I had to create a fun and lasting memory? I looked around at my nearby options. I was on the ocean, but I wanted to be *in* the ocean. I wanted to feel that I had a genuine Mauritian adventure! "Got it," I thought. "I'm going scuba diving."

I walked a short distance to a nearby outfitter who just happened to have a trip departing in twenty minutes. I showed him my certification card, which always stays in my wallet (and has no expiration date), and quickly demonstrated in a nearby pool I knew what I was doing. Then I joined five other people, plus our guide, buddying up with another single, and within an hour of the inspiration of the idea, I was jumping off a boat into the Indian Ocean, breathing compressed air, managing my buoyancy control, and descending beneath the surface, trading my view of Mauritius's beautiful volcanic mountains for its intensely beautiful coral reefs. Giggles escaped along with my air bubbles as I realized just how cool it was to be in the flow of trusting, creating, and experiencing an absolutely magical moment.

My friend and client, Sandro, asked me that evening, "So, Dan, what have you been doing since you landed this afternoon? Have you had a chance to get settled in your room?" I took great pleasure in responding, oh so casually, "Yes. Then I took a walk, met a few locals, and went scuba diving. We had a lovely afternoon together diving the reefs from a chartered boat." He smiled, knowing me well, and said, "Of course you did."

The point of this story is that it doesn't take a lot of time to create a meaningful experience. It takes presence and decisiveness. Within minutes, or even moments, you can deeply connect with someone, discover something wonderful, or learn a deep and valuable lesson. So jump in!

Prime time productivity

While you can use all the hours of the day, some of those hours will, for you, be more beneficial. I call this your prime time productivity. This is the time of day during which you feel most energized, when creativity flows freely, or when it's easiest to focus or move.

I'm a morning person. Most of this book you're reading was written between the hours of 5:00 and 9:00 a.m., over a period of many months. I'm up early, with a cup of coffee and an undistracted mind, ready to take on the blank page and synthesize thoughts and concepts into distinct ideas and stories. I love the feeling of being productive before others are awake. Yet I know that as the day goes on, my magic hours typically wane. I continue to be productive in other ways, and may continue to write throughout the day, or even achieve creative breakthroughs. But I don't count on productivity in the afternoon like I do in the morning.

How about you? Are you a morning person as well? A night owl? Somewhere in between? Claim your own prime time and protect it for your creative tasks and important assignments. As those hours only come once a day, make sure you are rested, hydrated, and nourished. Give yourself the freedom to focus on what matters most. Of course, you can aim to expand your prime time with physical activity, including workouts, walks, and stretches. You can bring more of you to your day. Yet remember, you can't be at your peak for eight or ten hours.

Improving Health—Promoting Mental and Physical Well-Being

Although we all get the same amount of time in our days, the condition of your physical and mental health determines how you'll experience that time, the quality of your contributions, and your longevity. Good health doesn't guarantee long life. We all know people who have died tragically young as a result of illness or accident. These are exceptions to what we know to be true: *better health promotes better living, greater mobility, stronger stamina and endurance, and healthier minds and bodies.*

We all face specific health challenges that may stem from genetics, accidents, or circumstances out of our control. Regardless of your personal situation or starting point, I believe it is our responsibility to become educated and disciplined to improve what we can.

Becoming your own health advocate is an act of self-love. It also is a commitment to greater service. You can't give away what you don't have. You can't model and teach excellence in any respect for others until you embrace it yourself. The good news is it doesn't take mastery to move the needle—just a commitment to pursuing something better.

Better is better

Instead of looking for the best diet, fitness regimen, or health decision, strive to make better choices. Liberate yourself from the requirement to do what's "best for you" (which is highly debatable and likely beyond your current willingness), and simply choose something *better* than you would have otherwise. When you grow accustomed to that better choice, you can then ask, "What's better now?" In this way, you stay curious and continue to improve without feeling overwhelmed by obligation.

Better health reduces negative chaos. As you already know, the more complex and less stable a system becomes, the more vulnerable it becomes to chaos. When you're healthier, you're removing potential complexity while increasing stability.

Better health increases certainty. When the uncertainties of the future arrive, the condition of your physical health and mental acuity will *with 100 percent certainty* play a critical role. Healthy minds and bodies have stronger immune systems and recover more quickly from injuries, surgeries, and illnesses. Obesity also increases certainty. According to the Centers for Disease Control and Prevention, obesity increases the certainty of many future health *complications*, including impaired immune function, heart disease, stroke, mental illness, body pain, and "all causes of death." More than nineteen US states and two territories currently show a prevalence for population obesity above 35 percent (more than doubling from 2018). The number of annual deaths attributable to obesity among US adults is estimated to be 280,000 per year!

When you commit to improving your health now, amid today's uncertainty, you are controlling what you can while putting yourself in a more advantageous future position. Better health provides an upgrade to every aspect of your life. Show up with a healthier you, and you're having a better time and making a bigger difference. You also inspire others to become healthier, showing the way and sharing the joy that goes with it.

Consider these four categories of health you encounter every day and that you can elevate with consistently better choices.

1 **What goes in.** Consistently improve your intake of food, liquid, air, and ideas. Better inputs will improve your outputs and outlook.

2 **How you move.** Upgrade your strength, breath, heart health, and range of motion with better posture, movement, and stretching.

3 **How you rest.** Become better at prioritizing rest and quality sleep.

4 **How you think.** Use the tools in this book and others to promote intentionally better mindsets. Please seek professional help for more serious mental health challenges.

Note that these are not four separate categories so much as inter-related components that fuel one another. When you choose better food, you'll improve your ability to move and think. Exercise and stretching release energy and tension, helping you rest and sleep. Better thinking helps you prioritize nutrition and fitness and rest with more peace. Better becomes better, building momentum and multiplying beneficial results.

LIFE MOVES FAST, but it need not be hectic. Learn to optimize your sustainable pace and expand your moments. When you align to better health, every day becomes a chance to make new and improved choices. When you falter, sidestep self-ridicule and quickly reset to choose better thoughts and actions. Move forward, remembering you deserve the benefits good health brings and the space in your life to enjoy them.

Next, let's move to the third transformation of Positive Chaos to help you turn what may create anxiety into an aspiring future outlook.

10

Transformation 3
From Anxious to Aspiring

YOUR HEART beats faster as nervousness intensifies. You breathe quick, shallow breaths while feeling an inexplicable sense of doom. You can't sleep, can't concentrate, and feel unsure of yourself. Tired and trembling, you begin to panic about what's to come. In fact, it's all you can think about.

You are experiencing anxiety.

Now, I freely admit that I'm not a brain scientist. Nor am I a behavioral therapist. So, with care and humility, I will endeavor in this chapter to discuss anxiety, because:

1 It is a normal human emotion. Everyone experiences some degree of anxiety at some point in their life. It serves us to a point, and we can learn to recognize and respond to it in healthier ways when it becomes debilitating.

2 Anxiety is on the rise.

**41 percent of participants across all demographics
reported the anxiety they are experiencing
is worse or much worse than two years prior.**

Impact of Chaos study

Also, when it comes to productivity and performance, consider this finding:

**31 percent of working Americans say the
anxiety in their professional life prevents
them from doing their job successfully.**

Impact of Chaos study

In addition to these statistics, we also learned that while anxiety is increasing for everyone, it is disproportionally larger for Gen Z (those born in the years 1997 to 2012) by a significant margin. So, in an effort to help all of us in the future, as well as upcoming generations of leaders, parents, and high-functioning humans, let's unpack and demystify anxiety.

Anxiety is a normal human emotion that stems from the brain; specifically, from your amygdalae. You have two amygdala, almond shaped brain areas about as big as the tip of your thumb, which reside deep in your medial temporal lobe (one on each side of your brain). The amygdalae were long thought to be the source of anxiety, as they enable your perceptions of anger, sadness, and fear, and the controlling of aggression. This brain region also stores core memories and plays a critical role in your self-preservation response system.

However, the notion that the amygdala is *responsible* for anxiety is incomplete. Your emotional brain, of which the amygdala is only a part, engages an area in your frontal lobe (cognitive brain) such as the dorsal anterior cingulate cortex, and creates "chatter," a loop of stimulation that involves intense thought, resulting in more emotion and, eventually, obsession.

Your amygdala brings up the concern, but it's your frontal cortex that won't let it go, which intensifies the emotion and keeps the chatter going. Interestingly, another part of your cognitive brain, the ventromedial prefrontal cortex, seems capable of quieting the signals coming from the amygdala—pumping the brakes of anxiety to an extent. If we can learn to engage our cognitive mind to properly manage anxiety, we may be better able to limit its unwelcome and unpleasant effects.

A study published in the prestigious science journal *The Lancet* documented a more than 25 percent increase in cases of anxiety and depression. Younger age groups saw disproportional increases, with twenty-to-twenty-four-year-olds experiencing the highest increases in depression and anxiety. This was largely attributed to the impact of the COVID-19 pandemic, specifically school disruptions, lockdowns, shifting priorities of governments, and other disruptive factors. Millions of new cases have been added to what was already an enormous concern. The mental health of the world population is suffering due to a huge increase in varying levels and types of anxiety disorders.

For the purposes of this book and particularly this chapter, I wish to speak more broadly to the universal human experience and undeniable reality: we all feel anxious at times.

Condition, Affliction, Symptom, or Experience?

Many people are quick to claim they have a condition, when what they are experiencing is a real, and appropriate, human emotion. The potential problem with this is that when people name themselves a victim of a disorder this may remove responsibility, amplify negative aspects, and complicate the path to improvement. Today, the uncomfortable sensations that come with dealing with life's challenges or unfamiliar situations are often quickly labeled and adopted as a part of one's identity by an increasing number of people, and particularly among the younger generations.

No longer do people say, "You know what, I'm feeling anxious about this situation." More frequently, they state, "I have anxiety." In other words, "The condition, anxiety, is assaulting me, and because it's my condition, I must conduct myself with extreme care and caution, or medicate myself to deal with the negative feelings. There are certain things in life I simply can't do because of my anxiety." My biggest concern with this approach is that anxiety no longer becomes a valuable feeling to understand and transcend. It becomes a condition to accommodate, resulting in a self-perpetuating, incremental restricting of life experiences.

Perhaps your feeling of anxiety is an indication you are learning and need to develop new skills. For instance, even prior to COVID there was increasing reluctance among some young people to talk with others in person, especially with people who are new to them. In 2018, McDonald's conducted the *Workforce Preparedness Study*, which found 37 percent of Gen Z "tech natives" believed technology weakened their interpersonal skills. Interpersonal skills, like any other skill, need to be learned and practiced. These skills include talking with strangers, asking and answering questions, active listening, requesting information or directions, and discussing differing opinions. These aren't easy skills to learn, and engaging in them can be terrifying at first. Yet, they are necessary if you wish to have a full and rewarding life.

Want to succeed in business? Well then, you need to take these skills a few steps further. Learn how to persuade others, make a case for what you want, sell your ideas and products, and handle rejection. Social skills aren't just about making yourself more comfortable. They're also about helping other people feel comfortable with you or with each other. You become more comfortable by focusing on others, rather than yourself. There's no end to the learning and practice of communication and social abilities, or the avenues these skills can continue to open for you throughout your life. But to learn them, you can only begin where you are.

To simply proclaim, "I have social anxiety," or use the term *my anxiety*, promotes ownership of the condition and its permanence. That belief empowers your limitation and makes you less capable of learning. Perhaps, change that belief and language to something like, "I am experiencing anxiety, but I'm learning how to become more socially comfortable and capable." This at least puts you on the path, while managing your expectations and stating an accurate problem—you need more practice.

A staggering 91 percent of working Americans say the state of their mental health impacts their ability to navigate chaos in their lives.

Impact of Chaos study

Anxiety is a fear of what's to come; a fixation on the negative or potentially harmful aspects of what may be. When you feel anxious, the future isn't compelling, but repelling. You don't want any part of it! Yet, despite your best efforts, you probably can't avoid dealing with what's coming, so you stew in the fear and keep yourself in a miserable and unresourceful state. It's hard to be present, curious, attentive, caring, and helpful when you're in your own head, thinking about impending doom.

The first step is to get out of the future completely and work on simply being in the moment you're occupying, fully aware of your environment. Look around. Take it all in. Breathe deeply. This one simple action can change your physicality immediately.

Rather than hoping to dismantle your anxiety so that you can behave differently, start behaving differently and use your physicality to change how you feel. Continue breathing and allow your shoulders to relax a bit. Maybe move around, stretch your legs. Swing your arms. Stretch. Pay close attention to how your body feels. By loosening your physical stress and tension, you automatically dissolve some of your mental tension. Give yourself permission to not worry for a while.

Once you have created some space and the opportunity to exist outside of anxiousness, you can start working on a far superior replacement: aspiration.

Aspiring—Your Compelling Future

The transformation from anxious to aspiring is extremely intentional. And, no, it's not just because both words start with the letter A. The reason this is so important is because both aspects have a direct bearing upon your perception of the future.

Anxiety is, as I said, a fear of what is to come. But aspiration—the *act of aspiring*—is about directing your hopes and ambitions to specific positive ends and actively shaping your development. You will strengthen qualities you desire while you transcend those you choose to release. As you progress through change and chaos, you strive for ever-increasing alignment with who you intend to be. You also become more capable, accomplished, and experienced.

This mental shift brings a powerful realignment with two ideas:

1 You have hope and expectations for a better future.

2 You have the central role in creating that future, which begins with personal responsibility.

Which Polarity Serves You Best?

People are often driven to discuss destructive threats to culture, health, world events, government, financial systems, food supply, safety... You name it! We are genetically coded with a survival instinct to identify dangers. And make no mistake, there are dangers, threats, forces, and injustices we can and *should* address. However, to fixate upon these challenges or simply proclaim what is wrong and hopeless is a fruitless, debilitating exercise. It's also human nature.

Negative conversations come naturally and facilitate quick connections with like minds. Personally, I am easily obsessed with political events and controversy. I am drawn into topics and debates, as I find both a practical necessity and moral truth at work in the issues of our times: important, entertaining, and with the potential to become all-consuming.

But when the polarity of your thinking is fixated upon negative chaos, you may become more anxious and less capable of thinking in beneficial ways. Your creativity may suffer. Human connection can diminish as you begin to see others as allies or enemies. You become unwilling to enter open conversations about ideas, so you miss opportunities to understand our world with greater perspective and nuance.

I recognize that we are all experiencing enormous negativity, but I believe there also exists greater, positive opportunity, growth, love, and humanity in our world. Today more people are educated and fewer are in poverty than at any point in world history. Cancer death rates have fallen every year for the past two decades. The exponential expansion of the world economy and communication platforms has facilitated deep connections. Technology enables modern-day miracles of improvement in auto safety, energy production and efficiency, and nearly every other industry. Artificial intelligence will improve the ease with which you accomplish much of what you desire. And entrepreneurs, artists, inventors, and content creators have never had more tools or platforms to leverage for their work and outreach to others.

You may ask, "But what about the dangers of technology?" AI could take over the world. We're being tracked everywhere we go. All our data is analyzed by governments and corporate entities, every single day!

That's the point, the polarities are not an either-or proposition. They exist simultaneously. You choose, moment to moment, which one you align with. You get to pick which polarity serves you best as a point of focus and intention for action. You then become an instrument of Positive Chaos, by contributing deliberate, intentional inputs to the moments you occupy. You create small ripples in the world, allowing them to expand and amplify beyond your view and understanding.

Most of the noise of the world and the news of our days are just a spectator sport. To create Positive Chaos, you must take ownership of what you most immediately control and influence, which is what you *say* to and what you *do* with the people you encounter in every circumstance you find yourself. Simple, well-intentioned encounters can have enormous bearing upon your world because they can amplify in unknowable, profound ways. Furthermore, your words and actions, your thoughts and expressions, the moves, plays, and color commentary you bring to your unique circumstances are all opportunities to shape or solidify who you are now and the person you are aspiring to become.

What Are Your Aspirations?

When I was seventeen and first started thinking about my rules for life and my intentional path, I made a list of desired positive qualities I would nurture and protect. As an active and acrobatic young man who juggled, did backflips, and was flexible, I knew how much physical activity and health meant to me. I wanted to verbalize that intention to my future self in a way that was both specific and enduring. I wrote this in my journal: "I can always demand *extra effort* from my body."

Now that I am in my mid-fifties, it's amazing how well that intention has held up. But extra effort also means different things at different ages. When you're a teenager, it means you can throw yourself around in crazy stunts. As you get older that changes, because "always" implies that you stay free of serious injuries. I've learned to pick my moments and improve my abilities. I'm more flexible now than I was at seventeen. And my form is also better when I engage in acrobatic stunts. But my real goal and future aspiration, God willing, is to be able to physically play with my grandkids. I want to be the cool grandpa who can still get up and dance, hop in the game, or pull out a crazy, unexpected move. I can see that future, vividly.

I assume that you have hopes, desires, goals, ambitions, and a hunger for improvement of some kind. You know that is within your reach, and you're using this book as a tool to help you get there. So, let me ask: Does your positive future outlook have general shape or is it crystal clear? Without the ability to discern your aspirations precisely, you may fail to recognize the pathway to travel or the progress you're making. The world becomes a blur of noise and nonsense, all competing for your time and attention.

Take some time to consider what your aspirations are in each of the following areas.

Character. What characteristics do you most want to embody? Do you strive, for example, to be more positive, more encouraging, more assertive, or more kind? Who do you know personally or know of who has these attributes? Name the qualities and the individuals you know who possess them. Take note of specifically how you perceive these characteristics in others. Is it a result of what they say or do? How they respond in certain situations? Now, work on modeling those qualities by incorporating similar responses into your life. You won't get it perfect. But notice when you aspire to higher character, you destabilize your current patterns (in a good way) and create the process for transformation.

Health. How do you define aspirational health? How would you feel? What would you do? What routines and behaviors would become easy for you? Again, who could help you, by example and association, to progress toward your health aspirations?

Relationships. How are you aspiring to nurture and improve the most important relationships in your life? What about casual acquaintances? Do you seek a few close friends, or a wide variety of people in your life? Do you aspire to meet people more easily? How do you want others to feel in your presence?

Reputation. Your life creates undeniable results and personal impressions. Over time, these accumulate to form your reputation. Are you perceived by others to be dependable, likeable, trustworthy, honest, fair? What do people say about you now? What do you want to be known for? Your reputation can be an attractor for opportunities and can create positive expectations. A solid reputation takes time and consistency to construct but mere moments to destroy. Can you describe the reputation you aspire to enjoy?

Achievements. What are your goals and ambitions? What do you aspire to accomplish, achieve, experience, and become? For many people, goals are the central fixture upon which they build their sense of self. "I am what I've done and achieved." Or, conversely, "I am not worthy because I have not accomplished what I once set out to do." Make no mistake, goals and ambitions are an important part of an aspiring, compelling future. I believe we need goals to pull us toward specific targets of an aspirational future. At various points in life and career, goals can be particularly beneficial. But they also have limitations. In Chapter 14, I will help you to move beyond goals and identify additional benchmarks for meaningful progress.

Welcome to Your Funeral

At the end of your life, whenever that happens, how will you feel about the totality of your one chance to be alive? Are you satisfied that you pursued what mattered, fought good fights, and loved deeply? What might you wish you did more of, or entirely differently? What will your last party be like, who will be there, and will it reflect how you aspire to be remembered? This exercise may initially seem morbid, but I see it is as the ultimate aspiration.

On a beautiful but somber morning an assortment of people gathers for an important occasion. Some know each other well. Others will meet for the first time, completely unaware of their shared affection for today's guest of honor. What they have in common is they knew you, loved you, or were in some way touched by the impact you made upon their life, so much so that even though they could be any-where today, they are here for this opportunity to pay their respects.

Now, consider the following questions.

Is your funeral well attended? Who do you think will come, and why? If you desire to live a long, full life and be well remembered, realize that means that, as you get older, you should probably stay curious, interested, and invested in people younger than you!

What is the general tone of the gathering? Obviously, people are sorry you're gone. They will miss you. Will there also be laughter, shared stories, and a general sense of appreciation others have for the incredible chance to have known you?

Who do you want to speak at your funeral? Pick three people you most love or admire whose thoughtful commentary, from their var-ied, individual perspectives, would share details and stories of your uniqueness, best qualities, and accomplishments.

What do you hope they will say about you? Imagine sitting in the back row, or hovering above the proceedings, taking it all in. In that moment, as the speeches begin, what aspects of your life do you hope they accentuate?

How likely is that to happen, assuming they outlive you? Is the life you're currently living congruent with the impression you aspire to leave behind? Are your relationships strong and special? Are you extending yourself on behalf of others? Do those who know you best know the best of you?

THE LAW of impermanence extends to everything and everyone, including you. The sooner you accept and embrace your finite earthly existence, the more fully you grasp the infinite power of your moments. As you do, you'll gain powerful perspective and lose interest in meaningless activity. You'll take your life seriously, but yourself un-seriously, transforming even your thoughts and feelings about death from anxiety to aspiration.

11

Transformation 4
From Overwhelming to Ongoing

MBARKING ON my performance career at the young age of twelve, I was petrified. So severe and debilitating was my fear that I almost quit before I began. As I practiced my juggling routines, envisioning the audience, my heart raced, my nervousness piqued, and my skills faltered. It's hard to juggle with precision when you're paralyzed with doubt. No. Actually, I'd say it's impossible.

I called my mentor, who had booked my first solo gig, and announced that I couldn't go through with it. I told him to get someone else. He interrupted my pattern by telling me he couldn't. There was no one else. Plus, I had made the commitment and must follow through. Then, he shifted my perspective with advice that continues to serve me to this day: "Dan, every time you do a show, you really do three shows." I was confused. So now I had to perform three times instead of just once? He explained, "There's the show you plan, the one you do, and the one you *should have done* and will think about in the car on the way home."

In other words, he was telling me, "Get over yourself. You're not going to be perfect, and that's perfectly fine." Just be present. Participate in the process.

Life is a process. Business is a process. We can inflate the importance of moments and challenges, seeing them as immense and unprecedented. In truth, they are simply the latest versions of familiar tests, and precursors for what's to come.

This chapter, and the transformation it will guide you through, is incredibly powerful. It may release you from burdens and obligations you've held for years, or even decades. It will enable you to turn novel, perplexing problems into more familiar challenges, gaining confidence and clarity to handle what's now and next.

When you're overwhelmed, you feel as though the pressure is all on you. That the test you're facing is ominous and original, that what you do next will either make you or break you, and it's now or never. But the truth is, it's not now or never. It's *now and always*.

---

45 percent of working Americans feel overwhelmed constantly or often.

Impact of Chaos study

Overwhelm Is Holding You Back

This eye-opening statistic from our study reveals nearly half of those who are working part-time, full-time, are actively looking for work, or are self-employed either constantly (15 percent) or often (30 percent) feel overwhelmed by their work or life situation. Here is what most overwhelms us and occupies our thoughts:

- Money and personal finance are by far the factor that leads Americans to feel the most overwhelmed (63 percent).

- Women (51 percent) feel overwhelmed significantly more than men (38 percent).

- Gen Z (1997 to 2012) are significantly more likely than older generations to be overwhelmed by their workload and fear of the future.

- Millennials (1981 to 1996) are significantly more likely to be overwhelmed by thoughts of money, thoughts about the future, and thoughts about their living situation.

- Boomers (1946 to 1965), and to a slightly lesser degree Gen X (1967 to 1980), are significantly more likely than younger generations to be overwhelmed by health concerns and news and world events.

When you think about the impact that overwhelm has on the quality of contributions, the ability to be present for loved ones, and the negative experience of living, the reality can be... well... overwhelming. Alternatively, you can expand your perspective to see repeating patterns that you can shape for ongoing improvement.

What Are Your Patterns?

We are creatures of patterns who exist in a world of patterns, including the lunar and calendar cycles, patterns of growth and development, patterns of learning, and patterns of conflict. These patterns also exist within challenges that are simultaneously extremely personal and entirely external and impossible to control. We inhabit different versions of our physical form, from the tiny body of an infant, through youth and adolescence, into the vibrancy of young adulthood, ever aging and changing until we find ourselves within forms we hardly recognize, moving differently, wondering, "Who am I now, and where did all the time go?"

Your job in this lifetime, within the roles and responsibilities you've adopted—employee, leader, parent, sibling, spouse, partner, friend—is to handle what's currently in front of you with excellence while consistently learning, growing, and enabling better choices and decisions in your future. Perform well and commit with effort and intention. Live, work, and lead by principles you choose and admire in others. Follow through on your promises and become more capable, dependable, honest, loving, and sincere.

Perhaps your immediate, pressing challenges always seem to preempt the larger, more noble and fulfilling desires of your ambition. But that's not what is truly happening. The day-to-day minutiae make up the phase space—the playing field—on which you contribute real-time inputs that reveal who you currently are and your present capabilities. They also advance the plot, and either elevate the game or perpetuate the same patterns, over and over again.

This is why the idea that "I'll make that change just as soon as I deal with all that's happening now" sounds reasonable but is one that never comes to fruition. Until and unless you make a fundamental change, the pattern you're using to handle all that's in front of you now is just creating a future, amplified version of the chaos you're currently experiencing. You get more of the same, in different forms and flavors, until and unless you prove yourself willing to change the pattern and get something else instead.

Change only happens in the moment you occupy, without any guarantee of outcome. Positive Chaos is an act of intention without the certainty of a specific result. You're trading perpetual chaos and familiar, repetitive frustration for something else unknown and unknowable. You shake up the pattern, or step outside a plan entirely, to inject chaos that is new, positive, and deliberately different and more congruent with a desire for growth. Instead of operating from a fear of failure, to avoid a known problem, or satisfy an existing set of circumstances, you act with honesty, integrity, and courage to try something different. Then you stay tuned and engaged to see how your prospects and possibilities take on a new shape.

Every moment you occupy and challenge you face is a new version of a familiar lesson you haven't learned yet—a test you've already encountered but not yet resolved in order to level up. Simultaneously, this current test is also a precedent for how you'll handle this similar scenario or obstacle in the future. Fail to give it respect and attention now, either by a half-hearted effort or by hitting the snooze button to skip it altogether, and it will make a future reappearance in a generally amplified and more consequential way to demand your full attention.

No doubt your life is full of recurring patterns. What follows are some examples that may seem familiar to you.

Financial

Money is by far is the highest contributing factor to our feelings of overwhelm. How you interact with money creates countless patterns that play out thousands of times throughout your life. Money is the fuel for how we get things done as well as a tangible manifestation of value. This includes what you value externally, as well as a tangible expression of how you value yourself.

Do you feel deserving of abundance and success, or do you feel money will always be scarce and out of reach? When it comes to money, how you earn it, spend it, save it, lose it, invest it, and give it away become repeating loops—different versions of the same story. Even the word *currency* reminds us money is not static like treasure piled in a corner. Like water, it is a force which remains in flow. How you participate in the flow, or current of cash, that comes through your life creates patterns that cut channels of repetition.

I can clearly identify at least five versions of a pattern of "past investments gone bad" in my own life. In each instance, I was motivated by the desire for a shortcut or quick win. I was entering into an area I didn't fully understand, and I felt a sense of urgency to do something quickly. It's now or never! And, in each instance, the investment became a total loss, and each time the lesson (loss) got bigger. It was as if the universe was asking, "Do I have your attention yet?" As a result, I eventually established these rules to invest by.

1   Invest in what you know and believe. Don't get seduced by the alluring mystery you barely understand.

2   When an immediate answer is required, or you feel pressured to move quickly, deliberately slow the process down or walk away.

3   Invest for the long run and in what is genuinely valuable, not in the desire for a quick win.

Relationships

In the story of your lifetime, you will encounter many characters. With the mindset of ongoing patterns, you may notice different people seem to be recast in familiar roles—new versions of similar relationships. These may be love interests, friends, or people who upset you, create conflict, or take advantage of you. Pay attention to the patterns of friends and romantic partners you attract and invite into your life. For some, these repeating stories consistently cast characters who bring pain and abuse, reflecting perhaps a damaged sense of self-worth.

You may also encounter an endless array of incredible characters who are inspiring, good, and kind. Their presence in your life seems to require more of you, simply because of your association. This has certainly been my experience, as I have been blessed with many close friends, casual acquaintances, and mentors whose admirable qualities consistently impress and challenge me. Not that they are perfect. The closer you get to any person, the more clearly you see their flaws, faults, and failings—their own repetitive patterns of personal challenge. Yet, as you choose your company, you choose your version of the ongoing relationship story: "People consistently let me down," or "I can always find people to lift me up." Choose people who stretch you. Earn their trust, affection, and respect by your choices and actions.

Jobs

What patterns are at work in your professional world or the advancement of your career? Do you find jobs that are easy or challenging? What criteria do you use to choose an employer? Or are you more entrepreneurial by nature? In your profession, are you constantly being valued and asked to take on greater responsibility? Or do you find it difficult to advance and deliver what is required of you? How long do you typically work at a job before you feel the need to move on or try something different?

Health

Do you see yourself as a healthy person? Are you adopting and enjoying patterns of thought and action that contribute to healthy growth? Or are you consistently facing patterns of disease and distress? What challenges to your mental and physical health continue to show up throughout your life?

Can you begin to see that these are not isolated instances thrust upon you, but different versions of similar scenarios, playing on a repetitive loop? Once you do, you will realize that the way you have been handling these challenges is insufficient to create real change. You must respond differently to transcend and change your current health patterns.

Three Shows

The concept of the three shows, first introduced to me by my mentor, is essential to any undertaking you face, from career opportunities to personal conversations and everything in between. It's also key to helping you make and absorb changes. Any time you do a show or show up for an important moment, there is your plan, your performance, and your process afterward. Let's take a look at all three.

Plan

Without a plan, forethought, or any preparation, you have no business on stage. This is also true in the performances of life and business. Now, depending upon what you're trying to do or accomplish, and the amount of advance notice you receive, your plan could be an extensive, elaborate undertaking. It could also be as simple as setting an intention about what you are trying to accomplish or achieve. Get clear on your objective and the qualities you want to embody, such as calm confidence, sincerity, or commitment to your ideas.

Regardless of how well you prepare, however, your plan will be imperfect and incomplete, as you're leaving out the most important element: the audience. Whether an audience of thousands or an audience of one, having human connection injects the unpredictable element, the chaos of randomness and uncertainty. How will others react or receive what we are offering? At some point, we let go of our planning and step into the moment.

Perform

The planning is in the past. It serves you but doesn't restrict you. You don't have to be perfect. Be present. Realize you have something valuable to contribute and do. Go about your business, bringing joy and uniqueness to the undertaking. Stay curious and tuned in to your environment. When something unanticipated happens, recognize it and respond accordingly. Keep it real. Have fun. Serve others. Follow through, finishing your performance with energy and attention to detail.

Process

The third show can be painful, as you relive mistakes you made or realize opportunities you missed entirely: what you should have said or could have done differently. Yet this is the also the moment where you have an incredible opportunity to learn and grow. Fail to appreciate and learn from your past, and you will perpetuate ongoing patterns and miss the opportunity to grow.

Many people make the mistake of skipping or shortchanging the experience of fully processing a performance after the fact. Their ego won't allow them to face the current "gap" between what they desire and what they delivered. They think, "I'll just try again and do better next time. Repetition will make me better." Not necessarily. The more you do something, the more you do something. Improvement is a choice before it becomes a process and, eventually, a result. Otherwise, repetition simply grooves familiar habits and patterns of perpetual limitation.

Accept the gifts of the third show. To the best of your ability, be objective without judging yourself, amplifying mistakes, or becoming defeated. Process what happened. Learn from what worked and what didn't. And incorporate your insights and commitments into the next plan and performance.

Next

The concept of "next" is powerful. With the understanding that there is no end result, and life is an ongoing project, you can reset more quickly from failure . . . and success. You don't let setbacks define you. They become immediate lessons. The bigger and more humiliating the defeat, the greater the potential breakthrough of understanding. Some lessons are painful, and expensive, but you get what you pay for! Every downside has an upside, and vice versa.

Success contributes momentum and validation, and also lays a trap of complacency. If you believe you've arrived, you unpack and get comfortable, while life continues to move on and transform. When things go well in your life you should take note and celebrate, briefly. Then move on. Next! Can you capitalize on your momentum? What is the next opportunity or goal that is now visible from the vantage point you've attained?

Cultivate the Watcher

Part of performing onstage is the ability to simultaneously act out the events while *perceiving yourself* doing so. You develop the ability to see yourself, as if from the back of the room, on stage speaking, moving, talking, and doing. This duality of existence—the performer and the observer—enables you to understand the impact of your actions as they happen.

This same skill set, becoming the observer, or watcher of your life, your thoughts, and your actions, is the essence of self-honesty and growth. In many ways, this skill is a prerequisite to the practice of Positive Chaos. When your life is all about you, how you feel, and the experience of living, you are immersed in the subjective and more prone to fixate upon negative aspects and unpleasant experiences. If you cultivate the watcher, you develop the ability and skill of incorporating a more objective view. You "watch the tape," perhaps not literally (although there is increasing video evidence of everything we do and watching video is extremely helpful in accelerating this process), but at least in the mind's eye and projected external perspective. You can notice that you are thinking negative or repetitive thoughts and ask, "Are these thoughts helping me now?" You see yourself go through the motions, speak the words, and create the outcomes you experience. How did you do it? How could you do it differently? Where are your opportunities to improve your patterns?

I've Never Done This Before—Or Have I?

When we perceive change as completely new or different, it puts us at a huge disadvantage and almost guarantees that we will miss opportunities and make unnecessary mistakes. So, please consider that what you're going through isn't as different and new as you think. In some, or perhaps many ways, you've already gone through this in a previous iteration. It is, in some sense, "another one of those."

But how do you face something unfamiliar and new with the confidence necessary to succeed? You find the familiarity by seeing similarities to other situations you've already been through—other skills and lessons you've already utilized. Leverage your past to be more present and create a better future.

For example, you're probably facing an important decision or a challenge you must overcome. Maybe it's related to your job, your family, your health, your finances, or a passion you feel compelled to pursue. You're not sure what to do because it seems so different than anything you've faced in the past. Step one is to ask yourself, "What have I done or learned that is similar in some way?"

By my late teens and twenties, I was paying my way through college by performing, studying business while building my own. I was constantly going into venues and scenarios that were new to me. Whether opening at a festival for a major recording artist, performing an after-dinner act for a corporate audience, or juggling fire on the ledge of a building (which happened). Big stages, small stages, and (most often) no stage at all. Figure it out. Make it work. This was exciting and challenging and taught me the skill of finding similarities quickly. It's about moving from "I've never done *this* before" to "There are aspects of this that remind me, in some way, of other situations I've already moved through successfully, or moments when I learned important lessons." By finding a reference point in my past, I could step into the "new" with familiar confidence. This same process has served me throughout my life as a student, business owner, parent, speaker, husband, and leader. We must draw upon what's already within us, rather than identifying what we are lacking and unsure of.

What you're facing now is similar in some or many aspects to what you've already been through. It's "another one of those." What experiences of your past serve you? What lessons have you learned that do not need repeating? What skills have you practiced that are needed now? You've been preparing for your future all your life. Step into the present with the confidence that you have what it takes to succeed.

You can also apply this idea to the way you view events in the world at large. Study history, learning the lessons of the past. Then see with increasing clarity how these lessons continue to repeat in newer versions. This reduces overwhelm by bringing perspective, revealing that we are part of an ongoing story.

What If I Did?

What do you do when you don't know what to do or can't seem to find a similar past reference? Have you ever felt stuck or lacking confidence, thinking, "I don't know how to handle this"? Maybe it's something you don't know how to do or say, a problem you don't know how to solve, a project you don't know how to start, or a question you don't know how to answer.

The next time you're in that spot, or if you're there now, employ this technique, which is so simple and easy to remember as it's literally four words: *What if I did?*

This simple question is a helpful way for you to transcend overwhelm and access the ongoing nature of your learning patterns.

For example, when you think, "I don't know what to say," follow up by asking yourself, "what if I did?" If you did know what to say, what would it be? If you allow yourself to go with the question, this disrupts your doubt pattern and helps you get out of your own way. Here are a few more examples of when to employ this strategy:

- "I don't know the answer." What if you did? What might it be?

- "I don't know where to start." What if you did? What would you do first?

- "I don't know how to do that!" But what if you did? What would you try?

What comes next may not be the perfect answer. But if you let your subconscious drive for a few seconds, chances are it will give you something that'll work well enough to provide momentum, or even a breakthrough.

Ongoing Doesn't Mean Forever

Everything ultimately ends or transforms, yet the ongoing story continues. What works and thrives for a time eventually doesn't. Relationships change and transform. Ideas and businesses run their course (remember the logistic curve) and, unless reinvented or repurposed, can lose relevance and utility. We lose our youth and innocence, lose jobs, friends, loved ones, and eventually lose our very lives.

This challenge we face of being fully alive while aware of our mortality is the ultimate expression of Positive Chaos. The same can be said for pursuing a goal, job, or challenge with extreme focus and determination while knowing your work will ultimately be over, irrelevant, undone, or become insignificant. The cynical view could be "why even bother?"

I think the secret is to take your life seriously without taking yourself seriously. Know you encounter countless moments of extreme significance, where you contribute your uniqueness, validate truth, encourage others, and fully participate in the miracle of life. Also know, like billions before you throughout human history, your story will end, and the world will go on just fine without you.

While we're here, we get to play, create, work, do, love, serve, and experience. We have the thrill and spectacular opportunity to contribute "inputs" into the chaos of now, shifting the polarity from negative to positive, and creating future, amplified outputs which will long outlive us. Some of your results will be known by you, and yet the totality of who you are, how you live, and the ultimate impact and influence of your life is completely unknowable to you or any earthly being.

To me, this is a hugely empowering and liberating idea. It frees me to understand that the reality I am experiencing is but a fraction of existence. Hardships become more beautiful when you acknowledge they, too, are temporary. Challenges become games and tests of your character and resolve. Joyful moments and the attainment of your intentions become sweeter and more special, as we understand they are but precarious, passing conditions. Here are ways to help you better embrace impermanence:

- Accept impermanence as a beautiful part of life.

- Take joy in giving, rather than taking or keeping.

- Just because it was doesn't mean it will, should, or can continue.

- See endings as transitions and celebrations of what truly was and beginnings of something else.

- Be grateful for what you have and experience, as it happens. Glimpses of perfect moments and remarkable times seem effortless and eternal, yet soon drift away.

- Strive to be ever more present. Live and learn playfully.

- Learn from the past, live in the present, and create the future—for yourself, loved ones, and those you'll never know.

HOW YOU handle what's in front of you perpetuates the familiar or creates something new. Either way, you establish a precedent for the future and will either perpetuate your experience of overwhelm or diminish it.

Can you see the patterns in your life that contribute to overwhelm? Which of your challenges and life events seem to be consistently reoccurring? Are they increasing in size and severity or diminishing in impact? If you can't get an accurate read on this, ask others who know you well, "What patterns do you see me consistently repeating?" Trust me, those who care about you will have the answers!

Once you clearly see the patterns, you can then interrupt them by responding differently. Do something you haven't done before, without an attachment to outcome. Inject Positive Chaos with new words and actions. You can start with something random and seemingly unimportant. At least, this takes you off autopilot. Then, having interrupted the pattern, ask, "What is it I really want? How could I handle this better, more truthfully, and more in line with what I value?"

Once you have attained this precious clarity, you *must* affirm and act upon your revelation. Resist second guessing yourself or worrying about negative consequences. Remember, if you limit yourself to what's comfortable, you deny yourself what's possible. Don't play it safe (and familiar). Be truthful. Act with purpose. This may be difficult at first. Persist anyway. Literally force yourself through the new approach. It will initially be clunky, and that's fine. Remember you can only begin where you are, and you'll get more confident once you experience different, and better, results.

Later in the book, I'll help you find greater confidence in your personal mission and values. But even now, you have a deep, personal sense for what is and isn't in alignment with your aspiring nature. So act with increasing truth and positive intentions. Then watch how your world shifts to recalibrate and deliver different outcomes and opportunities along your ongoing journey. You're well on your way to realizing the ultimate transformation of Positive Chaos: from stress to synergy.

SKILLSET EXERCISE
BETTER WORDS, BETTER WORLD

You will continue to get more of what you dwell upon. Thoughts, emotions, and actions begin with the words you think and voice. When you are feeling overwhelmed, you can reinforce that feeling with unhelpful words. Or, you can accept the ongoing assignment to improve your spoken and unspoken language. Choosing better, specific, positive words will reduce overwhelm as they focus you, empower you, and improve both your internal and external world. Even when it seems like you don't have a choice, you do. When confronted with hate, speak of love. Speak hope in the face of hopelessness. Speak questions to gain understanding. Speak courage when confronted by fear. Speak what is right in a way that seeks not to criticize, but to inform. Expect more of yourself and of others, and the right words will follow.

Elevate your internal language

First, there's your internal world. The world where you spend 100 percent of your time! The contents of your head. The stories you replay. What words do you use to describe yourself, your circumstances, and the people in your life? Are they words that state immovable, overwhelming obstacles, or are they words of hope, positivity, and self-encouragement? Do you perform a daily review of your faults? Or do you validate ongoing improvement? Although these words are unspoken, they contribute enormously to your quality of life and literally shape the events that will unfold. You attract more and become more of what you think.

Speak more precisely

Then there's your external world. Your influence. The words you voice. Do you feed negativity and overwhelm or voice hope and possibility? Do you discourage or empower others? Pay attention to your small talk as it conveys great meaning. Rather than put your words on auto-pilot, choose them precisely. Continuously improve your awareness and mastery of language because what you speak expands into ongoing patterns.

12

Transformation 5
From Stress to Synergy

TEAMBOAT ISN'T just a ski resort, it's a way of life! The resort offers world-class skiing on a massive Colorado mountain melded with a distinct western culture and a fun, family-friendly atmosphere. Not only is Steamboat one of my favorite clients, but the resort is also one of our family's favorite vacation destinations. So, when the owner-operators and my friends approached me in 2020 with a stressful situation, I was eager to assist.

With COVID uncertainty at its peak, Steamboat was facing pressure from many fronts, including strong opinions they shouldn't open for the season. To do so, they would have to come up with creative solutions to minimize human interaction yet still fulfill their vision to be "the friendliest and most welcoming mountain destination in the world." Plus, they would need a new way of training hundreds of seasonal workers to do their jobs, maintain the highest safety protocols, and embody Steamboat's essential values to fulfill their mission, "Share the Steamboat Dream."

These were stressful times for president and COO Rob Perlman and his team. Yet they strongly believed that there was a way to open safely and lead the industry through the chaos. After several meetings, I presented a solution for at least part of the challenge. We would seize this moment as an opportunity to elevate Steamboat's mission, vision, and values into crystal clarity, then teach that culture through video-based training that was tightly scripted, engaging, and easy to consume.

Instead of addressing the multiple challenges of the moment individually, we sought a higher vantage point of how everything fits together, at this moment and into the future. By pursuing *synergy*—connectedness and highest value—we asked, "What if there was a way we could elevate culture, produce results, and create a distinctive advantage?" Synergy is the opposite of scarcity. It's the belief that people, projects, and seemingly separate components can not only work together but *improve* together, creating a combined effect greater than their individual contributions.

Our team produced a series of videos for Steamboat that taught their distinct culture (mission, vision, and values) while providing interactive lessons about creating customer experience, elevating personal character, and performing a job in a way to deliver what is promised, yet create moments of surprise and delight for each guest. This solution was extremely effective, the season a huge success, and Steamboat further elevated its world-class reputation.

Stress can be a debilitating condition or a catalyst to reach for something higher, more connected, and far more positive and valuable. This chapter will teach you how to transform stress into synergy, which appears to be in serious demand.

Stress Effects

In the *Impact of Chaos* research study we conducted, we asked participants how stressful they found different types of chaos in their lives. Here's what we found:

- Financial chaos topped the list among all demographics (65 percent indicated it as being either extremely or somewhat stressful).
- Younger generations (Gen Z and millennials) experience more stress than other generations in all areas.
- Those in management roles experience more stress at work than employees do.

HOW STRESSFUL IS EACH TYPE OF CHAOS IN YOUR LIFE?

(by total, rounded to nearest percentage point)

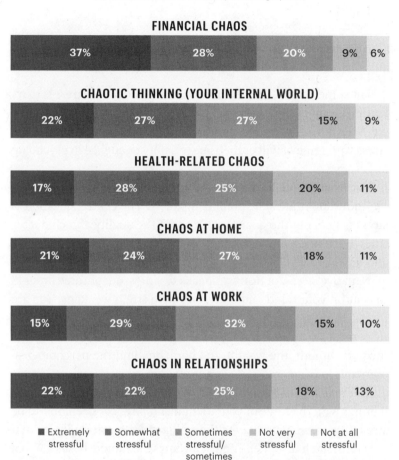

FINANCIAL CHAOS

| 37% | 28% | 20% | 9% | 6% |

CHAOTIC THINKING (YOUR INTERNAL WORLD)

| 22% | 27% | 27% | 15% | 9% |

HEALTH-RELATED CHAOS

| 17% | 28% | 25% | 20% | 11% |

CHAOS AT HOME

| 21% | 24% | 27% | 18% | 11% |

CHAOS AT WORK

| 15% | 29% | 32% | 15% | 10% |

CHAOS IN RELATIONSHIPS

| 22% | 22% | 25% | 18% | 13% |

■ Extremely stressful ■ Somewhat stressful ■ Sometimes stressful/ sometimes not stressful ■ Not very stressful ■ Not at all stressful

How much stress can you handle?

This central stress question implies that you should be able to endure some amount or duration of overbearing hardship or pressure. The *quantity* of stress is the primary concern. But although some people can handle enormous physical and mental burdens, others are far more susceptible to the negative effects of stress, including:

- **Physical effects:** body aches, fatigue, nausea, trouble sleeping, digestive issues, chest pain, racing heart, and sexual performance issues.

- **Psychological effects:** confusion, anxiety, depression, irritability, lack of motivation, sadness, escapism, and addictive behavior.

For some people, the default response to negative stress is to try harder, endure more, become stronger, or escape their current torment by indulging in fantasy or vices. They either meet the force of stress with force of will or they flee to safety or engage in psychological escape.

But what you need to know is that the "how much can you handle" question misses the point completely. The central question of stress isn't about the quantity. It's about the quality and characteristics of the stress and its relationship to your purpose, goals, values, and sense of self.

Negative stress, or *distress*, speaks to a pressure or force brought to bear on your mind and body. Negative stress weakens. You are forced through an unwelcome and difficult ordeal. You feel little control or purpose to the torment. Your challenge is to endure the punishment, the weight, the hardship, and the psychological pressure.

You may try to meet the force of negative chaos and the stress it brings with the force of your mental and physical strength—to be strong, be tough, survive. As the brilliant and profoundly influential German philosopher Friedrich Nietzsche famously said, "That which does not kill you makes you stronger." Ironically, and tragically, Nietzsche suffered progressive health complications, multiple strokes, and paralysis, lost his mental faculties at forty-five, and died at the age of fifty-five.

This popular, positive characterization of negative stress as being something that strengthens you remains irresistibly intriguing as a way to reframe our pain and trauma. The problem is, it isn't always true. Physical injury often leaves enduring pain, limitations of movement, and susceptibility to future injuries. Trauma leaves deep psychological repercussions, often lingering, lifelong scars, and may make you more vulnerable to future trauma. Psychological and physical abuse can be crippling for people, leading to patterns of continued abusive or self-destructive behaviors. Addiction escalates until it reaches crisis. Even less extreme, negative stress we encounter in life and at work can have a debilitating, progressive effect of diminishing our health, joy, and spirit. That which doesn't kill you quite often makes you weaker.

Positive Stress

Positive stress, or *eustress*, works to your benefit, growth, and sense of purpose. In terms of the amount of stress, it is enough for you to handle without breaking under the burden. Equally important, though, it is congruent with a desire, ambition, or a cause you value. Examples of positive stress include:

- physical exercise pushing beyond your current limitations.

- a course of study in a field that interests and excites you.

- pursuing a new skill or achievement of your selection.

- accepting a promotion to a job that will require you to grow.

- expending time and effort in support of those you love.

- working for an organization or worthy cause you believe in.

- stretching your faith and spiritual growth through study and real-life application.

- choosing to voluntarily confront a fear or revisit a traumatic experience.

Adjusting Your Stress Polarity

If you want to move beyond the default, or your current pattern and relationship with stress, you have three primary ways to improve your response:

1 You can actively work to lessen negative stress.

2 You can recharacterize the stress you're facing.

3 You can redesign your life and your professional commitments to find synergy, or positive complexity.

Lessen negative stress

This first adjustment to your response system is about using impermanence to your advantage. Just because something was, or is, doesn't mean it must continue to be. If you are experiencing unhealthy stress in your life right now, recognize that and resolve to change the pattern. Shake it up immediately by injecting Positive Chaos—intentional and new responses to recurring and familiar circumstances. Here are two ways to do that:

1 **Remove unwanted obligations from your life.** Get into the habit of saying, "I am no longer able to continue fulfilling this role." Or "My current commitments (to health and well-being, or to other pursuits) preclude my ability to do this any longer, and I must step away." Be grateful and pleasant but firm and unwavering. You're no longer the person for that responsibility. Let it go.

2 **Decide who you should spend less time around.** Who are the people in your life that currently stress you out when you see them or speak to them? How can you reduce your exposure to these people and the emotional burden they bring? You may need to break up with certain friends and colleagues. Or you can simply choose not to indulge their negativity any longer and let them leave you.

Recharacterize your stress

This response is not about changing your circumstances but about shifting your focus from a negative polarity to a positive one. This shift can change your stress level immensely and may make all the difference in your ability to handle and enjoy the challenges you are navigating.

My wife, Shay, for example, faced the monumental challenge so many others undertake of caring for her father who suffered from dementia. The challenges were enormous, including obtaining guardianship, moving him from Texas to Georgia to be near us, finding appropriate care, dealing with massive issues involving his house and belongings, and seeing him nearly every day for almost four years as his illness progressed and mental faculties diminished until his death.

Shay is an amazingly strong woman, yet the compounding stress of this challenge would have broken her had she not been able to stay focused on the purpose, love, and joyful moments. She set up a scrapbooking workspace in her father's room so she could spend time with him and help him stay productive. Instead of feeling like a burden, he felt like a provider of what she enjoyed. They often shared jokes and looked at photos of people and places he could no longer recall. Shay has great faith and the love and support of our family. She modeled for me, our kids, and our community the embodiment of compassion, strength, and self-sacrifice.

If you are fixated on the negative stress, you amplify the burden and pressure thrust upon you. You diminish your role in accepting the obligation and the reason why it matters to you. You become a victim of circumstances, rather than a willing participant and owner of outcomes.

When you focus on the positive polarity of the same circumstances—the reason something matters, the love you are expressing, or the skills you are developing—the stress you experience takes on different characteristics. Instead of distress, it becomes eustress, and you can feel more powerful, energized, and willing to do what is required.

Redesign for synergy

If you find it difficult or impossible to reframe your current stress in a positive, purposeful way, you may need a more comprehensive life redesign. But don't worry, this doesn't have to be a radical shift of everything all at once. It starts by transforming your perspective about life's components, how they align with one another, and the connections that create strength and synergy within the concept of your overall life pattern.

In my book *Off Balance On Purpose*, I make the case that achieving life balance is both unattainable and undesirable. Balance isn't what you get, it's what you *do*. You are balancing every single day, making constant adjustments in how you expend and direct your focus, time, efforts, thought, and money. How you see the patterns—the connectedness and repetitive nature of your world—determines how quickly you recognize what's happening, and how effectively you respond to challenges and opportunities, anticipate what's coming, and initiate improvement.

In that book I also present a model of your "Five Spheres of Influence": work, relationships, health, spirit, and passions (or personal interests). These five spheres encompass all that matters to you, how you shape your world, what you create, and the experience you enjoy or suffer.

Should you approach each of these spheres as autonomous projects, requiring independent investments of time, thought, money, and energy, you will constantly be overwhelmed and stressed, as there is never enough to go around. They will seem to compete with one another, creating the illusion that they are mutually exclusive. That is negative chaos.

The way to achieve life alignment, greater peace, profound change, and significant contribution is to understand how these aspects of you exist within a pattern of motion, represented by the infinite loop we've now come to associate with Lorenz's attractor—a model of chaos in action. This is also the same pattern required to manage a five-ball juggling pattern within the bounds of gravity.

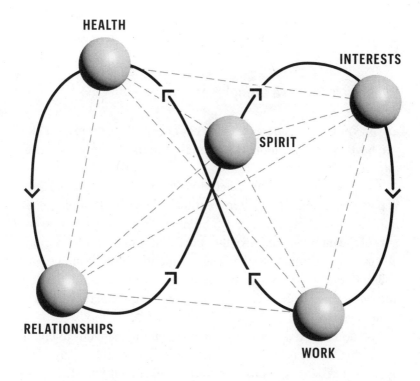

The Five Spheres of Influence, infinity pattern, and the ten "lifelines," connecting each sphere to the other. Strengthening these connections creates optimal life synergy.

Your five spheres are not mutually exclusive. They are intimately connected in your life pattern, each to the other. Instead of focusing on either-or decisions, you can simultaneously strengthen your quality of work, health, relationships, spirit, and interests, seeking synergy—a multiplied result greater than the sum of the components. The way you handle anything shapes everything. At any given moment in life, you are directing thought and action toward something within your scope of influence. And at that same moment, there are other aspects of you that are out of your control, in other orbits of motion. This concept and process is extensively conveyed in my previous book, but the important takeaway here is that when you seek a higher view and see connections instead of conflicts, you can transform weakening stress into strengthening synergy.

Synergy Is Positive Complexity

As you know, chaos increases with complexity. The more variables you have in play, the more randomness and uncertainty you invite into the mix.

Synergy, in your thinking, methodology, and life practice is a form of positive complexity. You are creating and inviting Positive Chaos into your world by recognizing and operating with greater awareness of the interconnection of the spheres of your life, or the various aspects of any complex system. You are intentionally expanding your ability to encompass more. At the same time, you become expert and disciplined to be present and engaged with exactly what is in front of you.

You don't have to know exactly how synergy happens to understand that it works for your benefit. Just know that synergy is a byproduct of better responses as you progress in self-knowledge and clarity of intention.

Where negative complexity fragments and weakens, synergy—positive complexity—connects and strengthens. As you move through life and business, your aim is to become more skilled, aware, truthful, and authentic. As you do, your responses in all areas of your life become intentional acts of congruence. You express the essence of your ambitions and values every step of the way. At first, you may find you are clumsy at this. But with practice, you will become more consistent and confident.

Synergy in Business

As I work with great leaders and organizations, they increasingly understand the value and necessity of synergy. Previously, especially in bigger companies, business structures and divisions operated in siloed organizations. That is, they were largely independent of each other, with autonomous leadership, management, operations, sales organizations, support, and human resources functions.

This is still true in many cases, especially in organizations that have grown through acquisition. For some organizations it is far easier to leave the existing structure in place than to migrate everyone to a new way of doing things, Also, these organizations tend to believe they can improve learning through the sharing of best practices, cross-pollinating ideas between divisions, business units, or various teams.

The limitation of silos, or autonomous growth, is that they make it difficult for an organization to adopt a unified and shared mission, vision, and set of values. Business leaders and employees are all busily pursuing goals and striving to win. But they may not be motivated by the same goal (mission) or playing by the same rules (values). Often silos result in enormous inefficiencies in the form of different budgets and teams for similar functions and goals. Similar problems may be addressed in the organization using competing technologies and people power. To understand the extreme of inefficient, overly complex, and disparate goals, or the wasting of extraordinary financial resources and human effort, you need only think about federal governments.

For an organization to adopt a single, overarching mission, and build the infrastructure and technology to integrate multiple entities, takes great strength and clarity. Usually this means enormous stress and difficult work in the short term for all involved with the promise of greater long-term success and synergy. But when conceived and done well, it is so worth it.

Short-Term Stress, Long-Term Synergy

Just as businesses have their silos, it's often easier in the short run for you to treat the different aspects of your life as separate silos as well. Perhaps you put on blinders and knock out the work, somewhat oblivious to the residual effects on your health, spirit, people, and passions. It must get done!

Or you isolate from others for a time to focus on health or spiritual growth, taking a necessary sabbatical. I get it, but I'd say two things about these kind of all-in commitments:

1 To achieve specific goals, keep promises, and honor commitments (to yourself and others), it is often necessary to focus disproportional time, effort, and resources into a particular pursuit. When you are biased toward what matters most in the present, this is another aspect of being off balance on purpose.

2 Even when you are focusing on one aspect of your life, you are creating synergistic repercussions upon other aspects. The result is that some of those repercussions will work in your favor, and others may create consequences that require future attention and repair.

Case in point: As a professional speaker at conferences and events, I've spent thousands of nights away from home as my wife and I raised our two children. This was never easy for me, and it is something I continue to think about, even as my kids are older and doing great. I recalculate the cost and realize the impact of my chosen career and path to success. The concept of irreversibility hits me squarely in the gut as I realize I will never get back those moments and conversations I missed.

Simultaneously, I realize the beautiful synergy of those days and years I invested in meaningful work and modeled professional success for my children. On many occasions, I traveled with my wife and kids to memorable destinations, transforming work commitments into family moments. We strengthened connections between our spheres by constantly involving the kids in our business, teaching them about our clients, and inviting their input on certain ideas and decisions. They also said a cheer for me each time I went on stage, even though we were often far apart. And I always raced home on the earliest flight, doing my best to be back for dinner, bedtime tuck-ins, or at least a morning visit and breakfast before school the next morning.

Synergy is a long-term pursuit and ever-present reality. Whether you recognize it or not, *everything affects everything*. When you do recognize it and incorporate synergy into your decisions and daily experience, you embark upon the project of a lifetime. Stress tests us all. It reveals who we are, how capable we are, and what we truly value.

CHAOS: Patterns of Synergy

After reading and thinking through these past five chapters, can you see how the five transformations of your perspectives and response system are, themselves, not separate, but part of a synergistic pattern?

Even though I've presented the transformations in sequence, building upon one another, the model of Positive Chaos—*Challenging, Healthy, Aspiring, Ongoing Synergy*—isn't five disparate strategies. Once you've adopted and practiced them, this model becomes an interconnected system and a new way of seeing, being, and doing.

It all starts with ownership: this is your life, *your* job, *your* health, *your* family, and *your* responsibility. You're nobody's victim, and there's not a single person more invested in your success and happiness than you. In life's game of tag, you're it.

As you respond differently, you contribute new inputs, radically transform future outputs, and begin to realize a new way of being. You'll simultaneously become less invested in exact outcomes and more capable of creating ever-expanding opportunities. As you let go of the need to control, you will become a true leader. You'll begin to realize remarkable results and abilities, as well as increased influence upon your world. Your life will take on greater meaning and purpose. You will begin to measure success through new metrics. You will become an instrument for Positive Chaos and a more authentic, capable, and effective leader.

Now, let's get intentional about the realizations to come.

PART THREE

REALIZE

---

79 percent of working Americans would trust someone more if that person could handle chaos well.

Impact of Chaos in the American Workforce,
danthurmon.com/research

13

Your Principled Path

NAVIGATING A JOURNEY by reading maps is becoming a lost skill. It's out of fashion, out of practice, and seems so unnecessary. Why would you endure the complications of unfolding, searching, discerning the best route, writing it down, or committing it to memory, and then (the most complex of all skills) *refolding* the map back into its original form? It's so much easier to use your smartphone's GPS, which presents real-time instructions, incorporating uncertainty and randomness (traffic and construction, for example) that a map could never predict.

As you navigate your life journey, you'll encounter countless billboards telling you where to go and what to do. You'll hear competing, contradictory ideas, broadcast with increasing intensity and volume. On your chosen path you will hit unexpected detours, requiring you to determine the next turn. You'll be presented "shortcuts" for quick gains or appealing distractions. And in the end, you'll very likely look back on your journey to realize the route was far less important than then *way* you chose to travel. What did your life stand for? What principles did you follow, despite the confusion and difficulty?

Before you can step fully into your power as a force for creating Positive Chaos, you must activate your internal compass and calibrate your personal navigation system. You will also benefit from navigating your journey in a well-armored vehicle. This chapter will help you do both by guiding you through a process to realize your values, purpose, and personal mission. I'll make this as easy and straightforward as possible. Yet it will require effort. Awaiting you on the other side is, quite possibly, more clarity and strength than you've ever known.

Forging Your Armor

In the chaos of life, you face a constant barrage of forces that demand your attention and participation. Some are important to you. Many are not. Distinguishing the difference and saying no to what doesn't matter are the keys to an intentional, successful, and enjoyable life journey.

You will also endure hard times, face battles, and experience emotional and physical threats. To bolster your internal defenses and repel the most destructive elements, having strong armor will be critically important. Sometimes this armor is like hardened steel, lessening the punishing blows and preserving your life. More often, your armor works like Rain-X applied to your car's windshield. Life's storms don't distract you because the rain rolls off, enabling your vision when others are lost. Negativity just doesn't easily stick to you.

Life's ultimate questions are not about what you suffer, or what you'll endure, but rather what you choose to do about it. What matters to you? What do you want your life to stand for?

As you move through the following exercises, give them your full attention and focus. The work you do here, if given appropriate respect and honesty, will serve you throughout your entire life in ways that you cannot presently fathom. It's not about choosing a career path, specific goals, or desires—although those answers may arrive in the process. This work is bigger than that. This is also a journey you'll continue to define and remap throughout your lifetime.

How you answer these exercises today will reveal a snapshot of your present, honest thinking and aspirational desires. You will learn the truth of who you are and wish to become right here, right now. However, these answers don't obligate you to anything. Values, priorities, and even purpose may change over time, and it is always useful to revisit and reinforce what matters most to you.

Also, although it may be tempting to simply think about these ideas, rather than writing them down, please follow through with the writing, either by putting pen to paper or keystrokes to a document that you save. Writing is where the "forging" takes place, giving ideas physical form. This one simple act can make the difference between a passing thought and a solid, life-shifting statement.

Let's begin with four exercises that will help you build your life armor.

Create Your Value Set

Values, simply stated, are your rules for life. When clearly defined and understood, values are the filtering system through which you see potential options and the guardrails for decisions, behaviors, relationships, and work opportunities. They give you clarity about what to celebrate and pursue. And they liberate you from alternative options that you can gracefully decline. Values aren't about claiming superiority or defining the "right way" to live or lead. They're about defining *your way* to live.

What do you most value in life? This might include character traits such as integrity, honesty, generosity, creativity, and excellence. Or this could be core aspects such as family, health, faith, or spiritual growth. Perhaps adventure or travel will make your list. There are no wrong answers here. Only your answers.

Your value set isn't an open-ended list of all you see as good. It's a finite set of four or five values that speak most to you. The goal here, however, is to develop a short list that you will easily remember and reference.

Let's take a first attempt at creating your value set:

Start by listing all potential values that occur to you. Distill this list to four or five core values that resonate most strongly with who you are, or who you wish to be. You may choose to combine certain values into one that encompasses both. For example, let's say you value creativity and excellence. Perhaps there is an opportunity to combine the two into a singular value called creative excellence that means something very specific to you, such as the attention to detail and distinction, infused with deeply personal, satisfying choices. Perhaps your value set list will look something like this (with your own distinct values, of course):

- Family and friendships

- Faith or a higher purpose

- Honest integrity (a personal combo as mentioned above)

- Mental and physical health

- Creative contributions

Next, write down why each value is important. Include what it means, and how it shows up in your life. Provide context and distinction to each of your values. Do this work in a journal, notebook, or computer file. Whatever suits you.

Last, prioritize your values. This may be challenging and also extremely clarifying. All your values are important, but which is *most* important? If you had to choose one value over another, as hard as that would be, what would you choose to be number one? Proceed with the entire "set" until you have them ranked in terms of priority.

Make Affirmative Statements

Affirmative statements are pronouncements of what "is." They positively acknowledge who you are and what you have attained. You are projecting into the future and stating your desire, ambition, or highest value from the standpoint that they are attained and beautifully lived. With these statements of affirmation, you are laying out how you know when you're living in congruence with your values.

You are expressing satisfaction that you're on the right path or have genuinely attained the state you seek.

In this exercise you will strengthen your value set by crafting affirmative statements. For example, here are affirmative statements that express the realization and active practice of each of the previously mentioned values.

Family and friendships. I am strongly connected to those I most love and admire, sharing mutual respect and understanding. I am there for those who need me, vulnerable to those who can help me, and quick to apologize and forgive when necessary.

Faith or a higher purpose. I believe in the existence of God, although I can never know the exactness of God. I strive to pursue truth, express love, and live and work with divine reverence, using my gifts to the fullest. Rather than asserting my will, I ask for help and guidance.

Honest integrity. Note here how the affirmative statement gives clarity to the "blended" value. I do what I promise, say what I believe, and operate in a way that is truthful and respectable. I admit my mistakes quickly, seeking humility and honest improvement.

Mental and physical health. Because I prioritize and pursue physical and mental health, I can demand "extra effort" from my body and mind. I regularly exercise, stretch, learn, and meditate. I age with grace, maintaining strength and agility.

Creative contributions. Through my creative work, I continuously challenge myself and benefit others. I have fun with this process and keep my creative commitments. I continue to improve.

Now it's your turn. Write down affirmative statements for each of your values in your journal or on your computer or tablet. These statements typically begin with "I have," "I can," or "I am." They are present tense, describing the active embodiment of each value you desire. This will give you an immediate sense of attainment and recognition of what it feels like to *live* what you express as essential.

Choose Your Life Models

While your life is yours to live, you don't live it alone. You're surrounded by people who provide companionship, guidance, love, understanding, and examples for you to follow. As with your values, you get to select the people you associate with, identify with, and strive to emulate.

You have unique life experiences, talents, thoughts, and contributions. No one else *is* you. Yet you are also an amalgamation of others. You've absorbed character traits, intentionally and unintentionally, from friends and family members. You've developed behaviors and response systems based on what you see as normal or what others consider acceptable.

Choosing the company you keep—whether that's active friendships or life models—is extremely important. Yet your choice isn't about comparison, but positive, desirable reference standards. It's easy to stand out as good or exceptional when comparing yourself to people who are dishonest or undisciplined. By intentionally aligning yourself with a group of peers, contemporaries, or models, you choose the company you desire to emulate. Some of these individuals will be people you know well and see frequently. Others, you may never meet. You don't need someone's permission to use them as a model. They don't even have to be alive! And you don't have to model all aspects of someone's character. You get to choose specific aspects, character traits, disciplines, work habits, and standards that serve you, while leaving behind what's undesirable.

Here is the exercise:

1   List three role models whom you seek to emulate, at least in part, in your own life.

2   For each person, describe the qualities you most admire and desire to emulate.

3   If you were to ask this person to give you advice or sage wisdom, what would they tell you? (Note: You do not have to ask

this person for advice to complete this step. I'd suggest you don't, at least initially. Instead, use your understanding of them and answer the question as if you already know the answer. You may be surprised to see that, in many respects, you actually do.)

Leverage Lessons Learned

Part of building your life armor and honorable character involves learning from the past without being burdened by past decisions and experiences. The life you've lived, the things you've done, and the choices you made were your formative moments and should be owned as such. Where you were victorious and handled things well, you earned valuable experience and a precedent on which to build. Where you handled things poorly or out of step with your values, you learned a valuable lesson. Forgive yourself. The past is over. You did what you did at the time, and it is done. Your actions at the time may have been the best you could summon at that moment, or perhaps you were testing options outside your values. In some sense, these moments are necessary to understand more clearly what does matter to us and why. Sometimes, to fully own our values, we must experience the effects of their polar opposites.

Here's how to clarify your lessons learned:

1 **Describe a past failure.** This could be a situation where you missed an opportunity, handled something poorly, and learned a painful lesson. What was the lesson you learned? How will you apply that learning going forward? What future situations and scenarios do you anticipate will give you similar tests, and how will you recognize them?

2 **Describe a past victory.** When faced with a difficult choice or important "test," did you step up and handle it well? How did that experience allow you to take ownership of your strength and character? How will you leverage that learning into future tests and challenges?

Whether recent or long ago, what happened, happened. The past is only an impediment if we fail to learn from it or refuse to forgive ourselves for mistakes. Past failures contain enormous value but only if we can learn the lesson. Conversely, past successes can become obstacles to future growth if we remain stuck there. Don't yearn for your glory days. Instead, see your past successes for what they were—snapshots in time and building blocks in a bigger mission.

THESE FOUR TOOLS, your value set, affirmative statements, life models, and lessons learned, become pieces of your life armor, forged through experience and honest thought. This armor enables you to enter future battles with far greater clarity and strategy, with resilience and strength, and in the company of honorable fellow life warriors.

Do not take your armor for granted. Forge it carefully, first in your thinking, then in your writing. Ideas held in your head are easily replaced by other ideas. Sometimes that means that the most beneficial thought is easily subverted by the next seductive negative thought or a simple distraction.

Please, do this work in writing.

Get it out of your head and into forged words of your creation. When you discover what and who matter most to you and convert understanding to written language, you will have crafted your life code. Once you do this, nobody can take it away from you. It becomes a tangible testament to your honest and noble thinking, a gift to your future self. Keep your life code accessible to remind you what matters. Make a recurring appointment to review your value set regularly, at least every year. Update as needed.

The Propellants of Positive Chaos: Purpose, Mission, Vision

In Part One of this book, you learned that the technical definition of *chaos* is the intersection of determination (your effort, plan, and desires) with uncertainty and randomness. Determination puts you in motion, and chaos presents itself along your path in both random ways (that you can do little about) and with general uncertainty (presently unknowable or the result of determined efforts by others).

Without purpose, your primary mission may just be to survive or endure whatever happens, and you will lack propellant, lose momentum, and find yourself surrounded by unwelcome and unhelpful chaos.

If you know and nurture your purpose, and connect that purpose to a tangible mission, you will create energy that fuels forward progress, greater maneuverability, better options, and the power to connect and collaborate with others. With the addition of an aspirational vision, you will create a precise, yet distant target that helps you sharpen your focus and improve.

I strongly encourage you, if you haven't already, to grab a notebook and pen, or sit down at your computer, and identify your values. Identify your rules by which you engage life. Then, make an initial attempt at creating your own purpose, mission, and vision statements using the following prompts.

Purpose: Why does this matter? Why do I matter?

You probably have different purposes depending upon your daily commitments, perhaps as a partner, a parent, a professional, and as a human on this planet. Your purpose as a parent or in a relationship is probably different than your purposeful professional contributions. Your purpose on this planet is an enormous question, one which may require many years of searching, exploration, experimentation, and emotional and spiritual maturity. Even then, the answer may continue to elude you.

With time, exploration, and ongoing awareness, you will gain glimpses of your purpose in two ways:

1   The micro sense: Your purpose in the moment, the circumstances, and daily objectives.

2   The macro sense (or the big picture): Why do you exist at this time in history and life circumstances? What is your reason for being?

Now it's time for you to think about the question, "What's your purpose?" This exercise may seem huge and intimidating. Likely your initial, truthful response is, "I don't know." Or at least, "I'm not sure." Fair enough, and thank you for your honesty.

To get past this, let's employ a technique I introduced earlier: ask yourself, "But what if I did?" If you did have at least some sense of purpose, what would it be? Write that down and see where it takes you. Purpose doesn't have to be complicated, and there is certainly no wrong answer.

A commitment to purpose isn't about a specific answer. It's about hanging with the never-ending questions: Why does this matter? Why do I exist in this moment and these circumstances? Your purpose will continue to evolve, change, and clarify throughout your life.

Mission: What is my assignment? What do I do?

If purpose is the reason *why* you do, mission is the current *what* you do. Each day you wake up and engage with life. What do you do? What are your intended actions and contributions? The answer to these questions flows from the answers to your "why" and describes succinctly what you intend to regularly make happen in the world. Unlike the movies, your mission, if you choose to accept it, is entirely possible, and takes many different approaches and forms.

To help you figure out what your mission statements are, here are some examples of my own missions:

I work with excellence, play with passion, and express love and hope to all I encounter.

This mission is about the way I engage with the world and the people in it. I see myself as an example in how I do things, my spirit and sense of playfulness (lessening the heaviness and seriousness of the world), and as an instrument for uplifting others (which is one of my gifts).

Here's another:

I write and create content and deliver experiences, enabling people to love themselves, believe in their abilities, and act with greater courage and confidence.

This mission speaks more to my work. This informs my weekly coaching videos, social media, writing, speaking engagements, consultations, and other professional contributions.

This last example of a personal mission may seem overly simplistic, yet it is almost universally applicable:

I make things better while making myself better, every single day.

This mission statement reinforces my commitment to ongoing improvement and reminds me that no matter the circumstances, I can generally find a way to contribute. Also, as this version is the shortest of the three, it's also the one most easily remembered and kept top of mind.

Note that in each instance, the mission answers the question, "What do I do today?" When floundering or confused, a well-worded mission points you in the direction of purpose.

Your turn. Give it a shot. In your journal or on your keyboard, write one or multiple missions you choose to accept!

Vision: Who am I becoming?
What am I working to change or create?

Your vision describes, in a succinct statement, the person you are becoming, or the impact you seek to create in the world. Visions should be compelling and aspirational almost to the point of being unachievable. You heard that right. You never fully realize a vision as its scope is never-ending. This keeps life meaningful regardless of age or circumstances and prompts you to continue to strive toward the realization you see and desire.

Again, here are some examples:

Through my life, I am an example of living with passion, giving with love, and creating with excellence.

I am transcending pain and suffering to become more powerful, more capable, and more influential in my world.

I am striving to create a world with less pain, greater hope, and incredible joy!

I am eliminating negative, debilitating emotions, and critical self-talk, enabling people to love themselves and become creators of Positive Chaos.

This work is so essential to elevating your life and influence, yet it can be difficult and uncomfortable to do. Remember, if you limit yourself to what's comfortable, you deny yourself what's possible. In this case, what's possible and within your reach is a life of greater clarity, meaning, and direction. Devoting a small measure of time to moving through this process will effectively upgrade how you see yourself, live, and make decisions, from this point forward.

One reason I like to encourage people to write down the answers to these exercises is because intentional language, like purposeful action, has the power to ignite change and transformation. Often, clues reside in our feelings and our responses to the world. Excitement, joy, and wonder alert us to the ideas and experiences that will fulfill us. Anger, sadness, and disgust reveal aspects we feel compelled to change. And if what you describe makes you simultaneously excited and somewhat nervous, that's generally a sign that you're on the right path. If it scares you, yet resonates with what you believe, that's a clue to far greater meaning and satisfaction—a life worth living—a positively chaotic cause to champion and create.

You may understand the value of these clarifying exercises and may be tempted to make excuses, default to the familiar, or choose to handle more urgent aspects of life, thinking, "I will get back to this later." These are usually stalling techniques. It will never get easier than it is at this moment, in the flow of your current thinking.

Do it now, ideally. Or, if you cannot, then decide when you will. Schedule a specific time in the future and commit to completing this work. Once accomplished, you will have attained and realized a more noble cause, higher purpose, and distinctive approach that satisfies your values while distinguishing your life.

14

New Metrics—
Gains Beyond Goals

MOUNTAIN UNICYCLING isn't for everyone, but I absolutely love it! For me, there's no better escape (or workout) than riding off-road trails through woods and creeks, over rocks and roots, up and down the Georgia hills near my home. It's incredibly challenging, as each turn reveals a new problem to solve, countless calculations of balance, effort, and strategic decisions. The sport demands intense focus and absolute presence in the task at hand, as well as significant output from legs and lungs.

Although this might seem an insane undertaking, I'm convinced (for me) it is far safer than mountain biking, as the top speeds on a unicycle are far lower than on a geared bicycle. On a unicycle, you don't have gears, and there is no coasting. This means you pedal both uphill and down, working all the way to claim progress whether ascending to higher ground or keeping your speed under control as you go downhill. Though unicycling may not be your chosen sport, please ride with me in this chapter, as I expand on this metaphor to discuss new ways of measuring progress along your chosen trails in life and business.

Going for the Goals

How do you currently mark progress? Measure achievement? Identify success? For many, the answer is based upon setting and achieving goals.

Goals work like this: At a certain moment in time, you establish future ambitions with specificity and exactness. Or, even better, you create timelines by which you will complete your chosen objectives. Just like JFK, who announced to the world that the United States "should commit itself to achieving the goal, before this decade is out, of landing a man on the Moon and returning him safely to Earth."

That example, and the ultimate success that followed Apollo 11's mission in July 1969, is offered up in countless books, speeches, and seminars as a testament to the power of a compelling goal and unparalleled commitment of resources to unite teams, talents, and imaginations to achieve the previously unachievable.

Goals can drive us toward amazing achievements. For example, this book exists because of a goal and commitment made to myself and my publisher. I promised to dedicate the time, thought, and resources necessary to make this happen, and it has! That you are holding it in paper form, or on your digital device, or listening to the audiobook is a testament to that goal's compelling pull and persuasive power.

However, if we allow our goals alone to define us, we may commit ourselves to ultimately unfulfilling journeys or miss better opportunities along the way. This chapter will help you realize alternate ways to measure your progress and enjoy the satisfaction of meaningful growth and accomplishment. But first, let's have a realistic look at the drawbacks and limitations of a goal-centered life.

The Downside of Goals

When you set a goal, you put yourself on the hook to succeed or fail. That means either of two options could unfold: you attain the object or outcome of your desires, or you ultimately reveal you weren't serious or capable. Consider these questions:

- What if your ambitious goals aren't realistic or possible?

- What if their completion is not dependent on your efforts alone, but upon uncontrollable elements and decisions of others?

- What if, along the way, you realize the pursuit of this goal is not bringing you the reward you envisioned?

- What if you lose interest and become unwilling to go further?

- What if other desires take precedence, or you change your mind completely?

- What if your deterministic effort meets chaotic elements of unanticipated uncertainty and randomness that change the landscape of what's desired or possible?

Would you call these examples failure? Or will you have made progress in self-discovery?

When you think about it, it's somewhat arrogant and audacious to presume that in a moment of clarity and goal-setting gumption you were able to ascertain the single best answer to the question of your future happiness. Still, I believe in the power and benefit of having goals. I've led many goal-setting workshops, and often I share the inspiring story of John Goddard, potentially the world's most prolific goal setter and achiever.

The Life List

John was fifteen when he wrote his famous "Life List" of 127 extraordinary objectives. As he was an avid reader of *National Geographic* magazine, John's list spanned the globe. His number one goal was to explore the entire length of the Nile (the world's longest river) in a kayak. He also set goals to explore other rivers, climb many mountains, learn languages (French, Spanish, and Arabic), instruments (flute and violin), and skills (including flying planes, skiing, snorkeling, typing, fencing, jujitsu, shooting, and milking a venomous snake).

John also wanted to bring medical cures to remote African tribes and visit an astonishing list of places. He wanted to study famous composers, read the world's most revered authors, write books of his own, marry, have children, and live to see the twenty-first century. All these items, and many more, John checked off his list. Accomplished. Completed. With each check mark, he once again became a beginner, and advanced to the next goal in an amazing lifetime of curiosity and learning. I encourage you to explore further and read John's list in its entirety.

I first encountered John Goddard's life list when I was seventeen years old, due to an unlikely string of coincidences. John was on a lecture tour, speaking in Chicago. He didn't ordinarily distribute copies of his list to audience members. In fact, he later shared with me that this was the only such occasion it happened. It was a last-minute, spontaneous idea by the event's promoter. In his audience that day, receiving one of those copies, was my friend and first juggling mentor, Mike Vondruska.

At this time, I had moved to Georgia and was about to graduate high school. I was already dedicating myself to an aspirational future, deciding to self-finance my business degree at the University of Georgia with my performance career. I wanted to expand my knowledge, my skills, and my experiences. Mike knew of my burgeoning interest in personal development, so he decided to send John's life list to me, along with a simple letter.

This one act of Positive Chaos, brought about by random events, caused me to think, "If it's possible that one person could achieve so much in one lifetime, then maybe I'm aiming a bit too low." Following John's example, I wrote my own life list, stretching my ambitions considerably beyond their previous parameters. Such was the power of John's influence.

I have since achieved a great many of those goals (graduating college, learning new skills, playing instruments, performing in bands, traveling the world, flying airplanes, writing books, becoming a husband and father). Others from that list lost their allure (including acting in motion pictures and hiking the entire length of the Appalachian and Rainbow Trails).

I now understand that such lists and specific goals are a snapshot in time—an inspired moment of ambitious announcements—predictions of what would or could make you happy, fulfilled, and satisfied. It's far more important to understand the quality and motivation behind the goal than it is to fixate on the exactness of the prediction.

Sometimes the objective is necessary and worthwhile. Other goals contain qualities that show up in alternate options that can be equally satisfying. In my experience, it is the opportunities and experiences that present themselves to me that consistently prove to be more exciting, incredible, and rewarding than my selected goals. This is because I have come to measure my life and business by different, better, more relevant metrics: momentum, trajectory, and alignment.

Momentum → The Force of Life and Business

When you are mountain unicycling, you must maintain momentum. Without forward movement you lose balance and simply fall over. Sometimes this means taking the long way around an obstacle or retracing a familiar path so you can keep moving. You create momentum by leaning in, or shifting your center of gravity off balance, in the desired direction of travel. This posture is necessary; but unless it is accompanied by action (pedaling), you simply come right off the unicycle. This gets especially difficult when circumnavigating a complex root system, hopping over rocks and fallen tree trunks, or ascending steep hills. Go too slowly through a moving stream, and the current pushes your tire sideways, sliding it easily across the algae covered rocks. So don't stop. Keep moving. When it comes to climbing hills, the key is to rest before the climb, or at the top. But, if at all possible, don't stop in the middle. Otherwise, you'll be walking the rest of the way up because you've lost momentum.

Likewise, when it comes to pursuing your path, pushing through challenges, and ascending difficult uphill climbs, your first essential metric is momentum. In physics, momentum refers to a quantity of motion and the impetus gained by a moving object. Without movement, nothing happens. Skills atrophy. Inertia weighs you down. Belief falters, and options become extremely limited.

You are a moving body. Momentum is your ability to move yourself and your initiatives forward. Motion creates the impetus, or motivation, to keep moving. For this reason, the momentum of my life, my body, and my business always has my attention, even above any particular goal. If you aren't moving, thinking, creating, growing, connecting, or exploring, then you are beginning to weaken, withdraw, and stagnate.

Momentum is more important than speed. If you are only thinking about getting to the finish line, you may skip necessary steps and diminish the importance of critical learning. Staying power isn't just about endurance. It's about staying interested, invested, and in motion toward your forward ambitions. If you can maintain momentum, you will eventually get there. Time becomes your ally, and if you can keep some momentum long enough, you'll eventually complete the extraordinary, where others have lost their way.

Because of this crucial attention to momentum, I am extremely sensitive to roadblocks, distractions, and circumstances that slow my momentum or stop it completely. What follows are some examples in business and life of momentum breakers:

- **Yes, but no.** "That's an important idea. Let's think about it, but table it for now. We'll revisit this very soon." Translation: nothing more will happen. Without a specific commitment to some action or plan, attention will drift toward more pressing matters, and momentum on this idea slows to zero.

- **The snooze button.** "I miss seeing you. We really should get together." Translation: we won't. Without a specific intention or commitment for a future visit, we have effectively hit the snooze button on our friendship.

- **Somebody.** "Somebody needs to handle this." This also shows up as "can somebody please take care of this?" Translation: without specificity, nothing gets done because those who would rather not step in see this as their out, and those who would take action may think, "I'll let someone else handle it so I don't look too eager." Unless you gain agreement as to who will do it, voluntarily or by delegation, you have just single-handedly stopped momentum. In general, confusion equals nothing happening.

- **The holding pattern.** "We're in a holding pattern until..." Translation: some element outside our control prevents us from acting. A decision or contribution by someone else is required to move forward so, until that happens, nothing happens. Don't buy it. There is likely something you can do to help release the bottleneck or maintain momentum in some other, adjacent way. Get ahead of your work while you encourage others to do theirs.

- **Endless urgency.** "That's important but not a priority. First, we really need to handle this urgent situation. We'll get back to that later." Fact: there will always be some other emergency. If you fail to prioritize what's truly important, you continue to perpetuate the pattern of prioritizing urgency and forestalling progress. It is possible to deal with the immediate while also advancing the intentional.

Overcoming inertia, the tendency to do nothing or remain unchanged, takes effort. To begin, restart, or keep moving through changes requires a specific sort of action. Here are five strategies to start, build, and sustain your personal momentum.

1 **Take the first steps.** If you're starting a journey, the length of the first stride is irrelevant. The exact direction is unknown. You have a destination in mind, but it is still fuzzy and uninformed by reality and experience. Start somewhere. Respond to curiosity with a commitment of your attention and intentional action. Just get moving and see what happens.

2 **Don't delay.** Wait too long after your first steps, and once again you are at rest, starting over. The first step requires another. And another after that.

3 **Find your rhythm.** Seek to discover a rhythm, a frequency of motion, creative habits, daily disciplines, regular appointments with yourself and others. Like the chugging of a train, the humming of an engine, or the ticking of a clock, momentum finds a rhythmic groove that is up to you to maintain.

4 **Check your course.** Now that you are in motion, you can adjust your heading. Do you like the results you're getting, or do you need to make a slight turn? You can fine-tune direction while maintaining momentum, rather than just slamming on the brakes.

5 **Keep climbing.** Rather than worrying about life's ups and downs, resolve that you are always on a slight, steady incline. You're always adding a bit more effort than required, seeking higher elevation, refining your approach and efficiency. With this mindset, you can take advantage of opportunities and are properly positioned when the steep hills arrive.

When you feel stopped, remember you're only one step away from purposeful motion. And when things feel easy, don't take them for granted. Continue to add intentional, rhythmic energy to the force of your life. Get moving and keep moving, ever aware of your precious momentum.

Up to this point I've focused on momentum of your life design, or "deterministic momentum." But this is a book about chaos, specifically Positive Chaos that you create and engage to elevate your life, impact, and ambitions. In that regard, you will begin to recognize momentum that seems to just show up in your life. Where is the energy and motion leading you? How will you respond?

Momentum you never expected

When you are in pursuit of something meaningful, you will likely instigate Positive Chaos you don't expect. When that happens, ask yourself, "Is this a distraction disguised as opportunity? Or is it organic momentum in line with my mission, vision, and values? And if so, what am I going to do about it?"

Kris Holm didn't intend to invent a new sport or start a company. He was just pursuing his passion. In the late 1990s, Kris decided to combine his love of nature with his hobby, unicycling, and took to the beautiful trails in his home city, Vancouver, Canada. This proved addictive, but also frustrating, as the rocks, drops, and crashes would over-stress traditional unicycle frames. He bent unicycles and popped tires routinely, and he quickly realized he would need to build his own to withstand the intense demands. He worked with a local bike shop, Toby's Cycle Works, to build the first MUni (Mountain Unicycle) in 1999, featuring a stronger frame and cranks and a thicker, knobby tire.

Kris's friends, who were filmmakers, wanted to shoot some of his more spectacular rides, which are breathtaking and quite ridiculous. When they shared his skills and story on YouTube, the videos went viral (check them out—they're incredible), and MUni exploded into a worldwide phenomenon. Riding the momentum, Kris continued to make films, and he started a company to make high-end unicycles for the burgeoning market. Kris Holm Unicycles (KHU) was a response to momentum, and the company continues to create innovative unicycles, components, and safety gear and sponsor competitions, teams, and events to support this growing sport. Kris Holm is to unicycling what Tony Hawk is to skateboarding.

I've had a chance to speak with Kris, and what I learned is that unicycling is just one aspect of who he is. At his core, Kris is an environmental advocate and geoscientist. He uses his platform and company, and the momentum it provides, to advance his environmental work and philanthropy.

Kris's story is unique, yet also part of a recurring pattern. Passionate people try and do things that create momentum and can take on a life of their own. For me, this took the form of performance, then speaking presentations, each new audience offering greater experience and new connections. By maintaining momentum, continuing to show up, saying yes to new opportunities, I've continued to learn and progress over time.

Where is momentum showing up in your life? How can you say yes to the momentum you didn't necessarily anticipate and use it to propel your ambitions? When you do, you are fully activating Positive Chaos.

Trajectory ↑ Ever-Upward Improvement

There's no coasting on unicycles, as the pedals are directly connected to the wheel. This means you're always working, whether you're riding on level ground, going uphill, or riding downhill. You're just working different muscles. Of course, the most difficult and exhausting of these scenarios is the steep uphill climb.

To prepare for these eventual situations, mentally and physically, I am careful to conserve and recover energy where I can and spend it efficiently as needed. In my mind, I've reframed the concept of "level terrain" as a slow, steady incline. Slight uphill, an increasing trajectory, is my new "easy" level. The constant climb. With this mindset, when I get to ride on flat terrain, it's like going downhill, and a great chance to recover my breathing and leg strength. A slight downhill is especially nice. A steep downhill has its own challenges. But regardless of the terrain or my particular performance, as in life, I embrace every ride as a moderate uphill challenge.

MUni demands you keep your focus on the present problem while simultaneously understanding what's coming, and your status, in the context of the overall plan. Are you preparing for what's coming, conserving and recovering energy where you can? Will you make it to the end of the ride?

Momentum provides energy, force, and maneuverability, which are essential in life and business. However, movement alone is not enough. The second metric to adopt and ingrain in your ever-present awareness is trajectory. Are you getting better? In what ways are you improving? Are you raising your personal baselines upward over the course of time?

Upward trajectory, or continuous improvement, is a critical element of the growth mindset and your aspirational future. It's also a far more important intention than achieving a specific goal. If you are not improving in some or several ways, you are likely to decline.

Just as with MUni, you will encounter both downhill and uphill sections of your journey. You can't improve everything endlessly. Skills will atrophy without use and practice. You get tired or injured, make mistakes, and as you learned in Chapter 6 about the logistic curve of improvement, you will inevitably plateau. What I'm talking about here is a growth mindset: looking at the world in a way that seeks and pursues the constant climb, an upward trajectory in the ways that most matter to your present circumstances.

An active, engaged, curious mind will continue to grow and expand, incorporating new knowledge into an ever-more integrated map of understanding. A closed mind can only protect or preserve what's already inside it while rejecting new ideas. Aligning with a fixed set of ideas (an ideology) may cause you to think in ways that are dictated to you. Rather than examining ideas objectively and seeing complexity and nuance, you may make blunt, comprehensive conclusions that allow no room for change. Is it possible for you reexamine or reject what you once thought to be true when given evidence to the contrary?

Imagine a timeline of your life, from left to right, encompassing the whole story from your birth to your death. Along that journey you have progressed from a helpless infant, completely dependent upon others for your survival, to a functioning self-sufficient person. You've learned skills, ideas, and ways to navigate the world to provide value to others while caring for yourself. You became physically and mentally stronger, more capable of solving problems, and wiser with experiences of success and failure.

A mix of confidence and humility creates insight and allows you to help others in many ways. You learn about money—making it, saving it, investing it, losing it—and using it for all sorts of purposes, helpful and harmful. You may encounter tragedy, addiction, loneliness, heartbreak, and depression, and possibly even spiritual transformation.

As you think of that timeline, left to right, ask yourself, "Am I getting better in some or many of these ways? What would I add to this list? What improvements do I hope to realize over time?" Here are some examples:

- Intelligence (acquiring knowledge)
- Understanding (drawing useful conclusions)
- Empathy
- Physical health
- Mental health
- Self-care
- Self-love
- Managing money
- Forgiveness
- Time management
- Communication abilities
- Leadership
- Being fully present
- Managing emotions and temperament
- Keeping commitments and delivering on your promises

Here's the good news: you don't have to improve at everything all at once. The mindset of maintaining an upward trajectory is one where you establish specific intentions for improvement now, along with an awareness and a broader commitment to lifelong improvement. You may not be as physically strong or athletically competitive in your later years, yet you can maintain your physical skills an impressively long time, while becoming stronger and more capable in other ways.

Alignment ←→ Ever-Increasing Congruence

Riding a mountain unicycle involves alignment in multiple respects. Obviously, I wouldn't be in the woods riding a unicycle through trails, rivers, over rocks and roots, up and down hills, unless it was congruent, or in alignment with who I am. I discovered unicycling at twelve years old (the same age Kris Holm did), so it connects me to deep satisfaction and formative memories. I embrace my sense of play and physicality, as well as my love of uniqueness. This is weird and wonderful and hard and ridiculous, and it makes me feel like a kid at heart.

Yet unicycling is all about alignment in the practical, physical sense. To do it successfully, I must keep my posture stacked, my hips in the direction of travel, and my lean and pedaling in constant concert. When going through an especially challenging section, alignment becomes even more critical. Instead of bending over to maneuver over a tough rocky section, for example, I must sit even taller in the saddle, as if my head is pulled skyward by an invisible string. Similarly, when going through challenging and complex moments of chaos in life or business, it is essential that we maintain and lengthen, standing even *taller* in integrity, values, and sense of virtue.

In Chapter 13, you gained important realizations of your values, or rules for life, as well as your motivating mission. You also identified a higher vision about the contributions you are striving to make in your job and life. While momentum is about movement and energy, and trajectory is about improvement, alignment is about ever-increasing congruence between the person you aspire to be and the life you're living.

Are you using your values as tools for discernment and decision? Are you able to stay committed to your mission and purpose, even while chaos abounds? Are you able to remain calm amid calamity, bringing your ever-growing confidence and abilities to the moment you occupy and influence?

Again, the goal here isn't perfection. This is about the realization of the nature of chaos and the patterns you perpetuate or interrupt and shape in new ways. It is about doing the right thing—the *true* thing—even when it feels like the hard thing, and then realizing it may not be as difficult as you thought it was. The results of congruent words and actions can be transformational.

Congruence becomes courage when you keep it simple. When you can stay congruent and curious, rather than playing the odds toward greater certainty and safety, you will fully realize your power of Positive Chaos. You can commend yourself when you apply your values with consistency. You'll also be able to forgive yourself when you don't. Misaligned decisions, thoughts, and behaviors will be increasingly unsatisfying, and you'll see those moments, perhaps, as tests you'll retake in some other future version, equipped with greater awareness and resolve.

Experience tells me it's unlikely you'll read this and decide to throw yourself into MUni as a new pastime. I'm fine with that. More trails for me. However, what *is* of primary importance is that you commit, right now, to applying the "new metrics" of *momentum*, *trajectory*, and *alignment* to your life. When you do, you will realize an entirely different sense of personal measure and accountability. You will set yourself apart in profound, inspiring ways. And you will attract others to your cause and mission, creating unexpected opportunities of Positive Chaos.

Legacy of a Lifetime

I was at the Nashville airport, having just finished a speech, when my phone rang, and a voice I'd never heard before said, "Hello, Dan.

This is John Goddard." That's right. The life list guy—the most inspiring human I'd ever heard of—called me.

Here's why. Six months earlier I delivered a speech in Charlotte, North Carolina, to a group of young leaders. I shared John Goddard's story and life list, and a young woman, Renee, approached me afterward saying, "Thank you for talking about John Goddard. That happens to be my uncle." You never know who's in your audience, which is why clarity of intention and alignment to principles always matter.

I told Renee one of my goals was to meet her uncle. She wrote John a letter, and that's why he was calling me.

"Dan, how do you use my story?" For a second, I thought I was in trouble, but I answered, "Dr. Goddard, I talk about setting goals."

"Ah, yes. The problem, I think, Dan, is most people don't set their goals high enough. They don't feel the compelling pull of future possibilities. What do you think?"

I was taken aback. He was actually asking me what I thought about goal setting. "Dr. Goddard, I agree, and I don't think they understand the power of writing them down."

"Absolutely, Dan, and please call me John. It all starts there. When you write it down, you take it out of your head and make it real. You begin to see things differently and attract opportunities to further your ambitions. Tell me, Dan, how many goals do you think I've achieved?"

Fortunately, I'd done my homework; I knew that of the original list of 127 goals, John had achieved 112. But I wanted to flatter the man, so I aimed lower. "John, if you could have achieved even a hundred of those incredible goals, that would be amazing." What he said next blew my mind.

"Dan, I wrote that list when I was fifteen. Surely you don't think that's all I aspired to do?" I nearly dropped the phone. He then told me his current list was over six hundred goals, and of those he had achieved 520. But he wasn't bragging about his life, he was asking about mine. "What are you working on, Dan? What's on your list? I've never met a man or woman I couldn't learn from." As the call ended, John even called me his kindred spirit, and I felt simultaneously empowered and challenged to elevate my life and ambitions.

John and I became very close. When speaking near Los Angeles, I would visit with him and his wife, Carol. We went hiking together several times, and John came to Georgia to spend time with my family. On John's eightieth birthday and the anniversary of his number one goal, we returned to Egypt together to celebrate. We weren't in a kayak. We were on a cruise ship. But it was still very cool! At the end of every conversation or adventure, he never said goodbye. "In our family, Dan, we say, 'To be continued.'"

I'll never forget the day John called me in Atlanta. I was aware of his battle with cancer. He was suffering, yet still full of joy. In the car with my wife, we had a wonderful conversation, traveling the familiar circuit of updates, thoughts on the world, and what was *really* important. At the end of that call, John simply said to me, "Goodbye, Dan." I hung up the phone and burst into tears. Shay asked what happened, and I said simply, "John Goddard just said goodbye." She understood immediately.

When John passed away, Carol called. "Dan, John's wish was that you, if you are open to it, officiate his celebration of life ceremony. Will you do it, please?"

Of course, I said, "Yes! Absolutely!" This was an amazing honor. But I tell you this story to now ask you to imagine that happening *from the perspective* of the seventeen-year-old young man who first learned, upon opening up a random letter from his mentor, that this man, John Goddard, even existed!

I could have never, ever contemplated such an occurrence in my life, much less set it as an intention. Or a goal. This is absolute proof to me that the most meaningful opportunities, relationships, and moments of life come not because you sought them *exactly*, but because, on your way toward meaningful pursuits of your intention, you were paying attention, in alignment with your values, and open to new invitations along the way.

In the audience at John's celebration of life were family members, fellow adventurers, educators, and accomplished leaders from around the globe. Everyone said different versions of the same thing: "John made me feel more special, capable, and important. John called me his kindred spirit." Apparently, he said that to *everybody*. And you know what? He meant it.

SO, YES, set big goals of deterministic intention. Life is fun that way. You get to decide, dream, dare, and do! What's on your list? Have you written it down? Are your goals big enough to compel you into action?

Then, having set your ambitions in motion, resolve to play the *bigger game*. Stay curious and open to what you could never expect or design. Maintain momentum, dodging impediments that could drain your energy and desire. Improve yourself in multiple ways, committing to a constant, upward, lifelong trajectory. And as you live, grow, age, and ultimately transition, stretch toward greater alignment, so that those who knew you will carry you in their hearts and live by your example.

You will never know the full impact of your life. Nor will it be known by the people who know you! The amplified impact of your inputs, words, actions, and contributions will extend far beyond your understanding or awareness. The next chapter will help you maximize this superpower.

15

Incredible Influence and Positive Disruption

IKE LORENZ'S observation about the weather and the butterfly effect, it doesn't take much to make an enormous difference. What it takes is *you*. Congruent, curious, intentional, brave, imperfect you.

In this chapter, I will help you identify and claim your superpowers and apply them in specific ways to realize immediate and long-lasting influence. Think Peter Parker after the spider bite. Something has happened, and you know you're changing on the inside. But you don't yet know how to channel the energy, hone the skills, and act with courage and purpose. Soon you will. And once you start using these skills and techniques, you will become a full-fledged instrument of Positive Chaos, disrupting your world for good.

Do you fully comprehend the power of your words and actions— how the little things can change everything?

Even if you understand this concept intellectually, you almost certainly undervalue your influence. Perhaps you feel that you're just one person in a sea of humanity, facing insurmountable challenges and unceasing chaos. Plus, you know you have some major flaws and embarrassing secrets. You've had some great moments, but you've also done some things you are not proud of. You're goofy, silly, and not nearly confident enough to take charge. You get flustered and

221

overwhelmed, especially when all the attention is on you. And then there's your dark side, which you hide from just about everybody. "No," you think, "if someone is going to change the world for the better, *it's certainly not me.*" So, instead, you may choose to hang back and observe, waiting for someone else to step in and save the day.

We all tend to diminish our own significance, and that's understandable. Looking out from the cockpits of our minds and the experiences of our senses, we presume everyone else has it all together, or at least a better handle on things than we do. That's because we're not aware of the chatter of everyone else's minds—their doubts, fears, and secrets. We see strengths and qualities in others we believe we don't possess, and we suppose those attributes make all the difference.

This chapter is about realizing you do have incredible powers that have not yet been fully activated. Your ability to influence is both universal and unique to you, given your specific strengths, talents, personality, and life situation. Every day, you venture into the world and encounter people who are directly or indirectly impacted by your potential inputs.

As you progress on the journey of building greater congruence, your influence exponentially expands. Yet, you don't have to be perfect, or free of contradictions, to unleash amazing influence. You will always have flaws. Of course, you will fall short of your aspirational values. You will struggle inwardly (overcoming limiting thoughts and doubts) and outwardly (making obvious mistakes). You're human, and your humanity, just like Spider-Man's, helps you connect to others in authentic, real ways. That you are striving, growing, and learning bolsters your credibility and also makes you likeable, real, and interesting.

Activate Your Influence

"Social media influencer" is, according to research, one of the most desirable professions of Gen Z. A 2019 study of children aged eleven to sixteen in the United Kingdom found one in five youths aspired to be one. The thought of having a large following, recognition, and endorsement deals is enormously appealing to young people, and this trend seems to be rapidly rising. In 2022, a study found that 45 percent of Gen Z creators had ambitions to own a business posting content online.

But you don't need a huge audience to have influence. You need a life, and you already have one. Consider the powerful, interconnected platform you live on every single day. You are already an influencer in your circles of family, friends, school, or work colleagues. You are even an influencer among the strangers you encounter. Believe it! The way you live, work, speak, and interact can lift others or discourage them, raise standards or lower them. You can add or subtract joy and meaning from the world in which you live.

To activate your influencer power, first you need to acknowledge that it exists, regardless of your social standing, earnings, or position. Influence doesn't just reside in the big moments, when you're basking in your achievements and greatest qualities. You may have the most influence when you're dealing with difficulty or moving through an ordinary day.

Second, you must choose to activate influence. If you remain silent or disengaged, you remain an observer. A lack of contribution on your part will convey agreement, compliance, or indifference. True, not every situation you encounter requires your fully engaged participation. That would be exhausting! Yet, as you develop your confidence and clarify your intentions, you can choose to engage with precision and deliver something of value to encourage someone, compel action, take a stand for what you believe, or simply validate the attributes you most admire in others. These small, but purposeful actions have the potential to create incredible impact and consequence.

Most of your influence is unknowable. Yet one day, when you least expect it, someone will come up to you and say, "The way I saw you handle that situation caused me to think differently," or, "What you said to me made me feel so much better," or, "Because of your example, I decided to do this."

Did you catch that? What you say and do and how you handle your life can directly influence what others think, feel, and do in their lives.

And here's the real secret: influence expands with intention. Once you own it and treat your words and example with dignity, you expand your platform and elevate your life.

Take Your Life Seriously Without Taking Yourself Seriously

One way to bolster your influence is to take your life seriously while simultaneously taking yourself less seriously. You are the captain of your life. Choosing, doing, speaking. Yet, you are also a transient soul in this temporary existence, like billions before you and billions more to come. After you're gone, your mark on people and places will continue to echo yet fade over time.

So, what is life about? What will you, as the sole captain of your body, mind, words, and causes, choose to do? What will you champion? Or will you just go along, bide your time, and serve your personal needs?

I believe we are called to participate in the flow of goodness, driven by faith, principle, or both. There is a right way to treat or speak to a fellow human being. Own your actions. Take humble pride in your creations. Value love and joy over stuff and status. Play in this magical world, demonstrating to others a beautiful way to do it because you can't do good without feeling good, or be pleasant without having a more pleasant experience. By striving for virtue, you attract virtuous people including, God willing, a soulmate or dear companions to share your journey.

Kindness, generosity, discipline, and hard work all exemplify noble virtues. And they all gift the practitioner far more than they cost, resulting in trustworthy friends, a richer life, better outcomes, and a self-satisfaction that cannot be stolen or bought. When you know this in your core self, you realize that goodness is not selfless, but self-serving. Being good brings you good, inside and out.

Others may reject virtues and still obtain what they seek, whether that's money, attention, fame, or status. Often, these things don't last long because they are transient. And those who obtain them never fully enjoy them because they are trapped in the lonely cockpit of their mind, alone and apart in a precarious story of plunder.

Joy comes from knowing that you are okay with you. Be present in the life you have. The next sentence that leaves your lips. The smile you share with a stranger. Choices become victories because even when it's the tough thing, it's the right thing. So, champion good. Love everyone, and don't take yourself so seriously. In this way, you will become a powerful, positive disruptor.

Be a Positive Disruptor

Let's go back to the Lorenz model for a moment. Remember how it shows us repeating patterns of similar "loops" (choices and scenarios) on various planes? When it comes to your daily experience and the power of your influence, think of these as simultaneous planes of potential reality. Like the Marvel Multiverse, there isn't just one version of what *is*, but infinite concurrently existing options.

Most of your choices about how you interpret the world and respond to it have been automatic. I see what I see. I respond how I must. It is *this way*, which means I choose to say or do *this*. These patterns are honed from past experiences and subconsciously designed to keep you safe and make your future more predictable. And, because present inputs create amplified future outputs, your consistent responses create more of the same, which will show up in some future way as another version of your loop—a similar (usually bigger) challenge, or new versions of the routine, enjoyable, satisfying, and disappointing. This only reinforces your perception: that's just how life is, and what happens generally keeps happening.

But what if predictability wasn't your aim? What if, instead, you saw yourself as an agent of Positive Chaos, intentionally disrupting the automatic to jump the tracks of familiarity and create new experiences and different results for yourself and others? If you were less concerned about controlling what happens, you might be more inclined to instigate unknowable possibilities. Can you begin to imagine a life of adventure, curiosity, and mischievous good?

Because little things change everything, positive disruptions don't have to be sizable to have an influence. A smile to a stranger, recognition of a previously overlooked detail, or the offering of an insightful question or compliment can be enough to wobble reality from the familiar and create a moment of truth and connection. A single, courageous, congruent act can instigate exponential change. Your secret mission, apart from your job or task list, is to look for little things that may make the big difference. This intention, applied over time, can radically change your world for the better. It's also a ton of fun.

Choosing to disrupt the flow of what is easy or acceptable may initially slow your progress. You may need to examine and address some deeply held behaviors and patterns that are no longer serving you. This may include, as it did in my life, addressing addictive behaviors. To disrupt those behaviors, I had to seek help, go through a process of self-examination, and embark on a program that took priority over other goals and ambitions. This single disruption was among the most challenging undertakings of my life. Ultimately, it was also among the most beneficial and important, as it brought me into far greater alignment with what is valuable, true, and important for me. This is the essential work of your lifetime. You may postpone this work in the short term, but you risk perpetuating dysfunctional patterns. Or you can address it, do the work, and elevate every aspect of what's to come.

If you choose to be a positive disruptor, you will also notice how this impacts others. Some will be inspired by your approach and compelled to follow your lead. You will attract people of similar principles and perspectives who appreciate and value your work, words, and way of being. This may lead to incredible, unforeseen opportunities, both personal and professional, which will enrich your life immensely.

You also may notice how your chosen path has the opposite effect upon others. Your quest will act as a mirror, reflecting their unwillingness to act, change, or place principles above immediate convenience. You may drift away from people you were once close to, at least for a time. Do not let this disappoint you. You intend no judgment, and you don't think of yourself as better than someone else. You want to *better yourself* over time. Stick to it. It will be hard but so rewarding.

Like an inventor or artist, tinkering with an evolving work of creation, elevate your process and integrity of the work. Instead of seeking certainty, choose wonder, thinking, "I wonder what will happen if I do this." Then, try it and see. That's Positive Chaos in action.

Let's begin with these easy, yet powerful ways you can become a positive disruptor.

Give encouragement

Remember a moment when you were ready to give up or lacked confidence, and someone's encouragement made all the difference to you. Encouragement is a powerful force that can transform belief, ability, and results. Your encouragement can bring people out of self-doubt and propel them into action. With encouragement you can change someone's life through the power of your words.

Here are three suggestions that can make the greatest impact:

1 **Encourage with passion.** As you encourage someone, convey your belief in them, and bring emotion. If they don't yet feel it within themselves, let them feel it from you.

2 **Name their strengths.** When you identify the qualities someone possesses, or attributes you admire in them, you strengthen their strengths. Think of this as flipping a switch inside their belief system to activate full power.

3 **Amplify the upside.** Many of us constantly weigh the pros and cons, and we get stuck between why we should or shouldn't. If you can, help others to understand how a short-term risk or effort now will change the impact and quality of their life forever. Be specific. Help them see a positive future with crystal clarity.

Encouragement costs you nothing yet can be priceless in its value. Who will you encourage today?

Pursue the truth

Are you withholding your ideas, beliefs, and perspectives for fear of criticism or punishment? Are you unwilling to learn the truth for fear you may need to change? Do you hesitate to tell the truth for fear you'll be judged or embarrassed? It's never easy to express your opinions and ideas. And today's climate has only increased that difficulty and fear. Cancel culture isn't just impacting celebrities. It also affects regular people and our daily interactions.

Like Indiana Jones in the Temple of Doom, we're navigating life with precarious steps for fear we'll trigger deadly darts of judgment or the wrecking ball of ridicule. It's easier to self-censor and say nothing than to say the wrong thing, even unwittingly. So, even among trusted friends, we have learned to feel for agreement and avoid areas of potential conflict.

Here are three things to understand about how truth can work as a positive disruptor:

1 **Truth triggers a response.** When what you say you want shows up as an opportunity, accept it, or reveal you've been untruthful. When you learn you've been deceived you must not only confront the truth, but also, directly, or indirectly, the deception. When you see something beautiful or admirable you say, "That is beautiful." Or, "I admire your work." And when you see something wrong or awful, you say so, or at least refuse to lie.

2 **Truth triggers an awareness of your faults.** This can prompt learning, humility, short-term corrections, and long-term improvements. Or truth can trigger self-criticism, embarrassment, or an escape attempt to outrun your own awareness.

3 **What are you pretending not to know?** What do you know to be true, yet are unwilling to say or do? When you encounter what is undeniable, what will it trigger in you?

Cancelled conversations prevent us from exploring and incorporating new perspectives, asking well-intended questions, or sharing ideas, experiences, and factual information. Without free expression, we can't build bridges between views or empathize with others' realities.

Do you want to increase your value and effectiveness as a leader within your family or circles of influence? Today that requires both elevated skills and increased courage and some specific strategies such as these:

- Learn to listen to others without becoming agitated and defensive.

- Express your ideas with patience and exactness.

- Avoid familiar "talking points." You gain greater influence when you use your own words, rather than repeating those of someone else.

- Present questions instead of definitive answers, and genuinely listen to the other person's responses.

- Value the person even if you hold a different view.

- Have the courage to start a meaningful conversation, ask a clarifying question, or inject an alternate, truthful opinion. Use phrases like, "Have you considered?" or "Were you aware?" to soften the impact of challenging new information.

- Remain calm and curious, even when you hold deep convictions. Stand tall in your beliefs without belittling others.

- Have the courage to say, "I see it differently," or agree to leave an issue unsettled and a friendship intact.

Self-awareness and honesty are skills we develop over time and throughout life. As you become more truthful, you tolerate less self-deceit and manipulation. You'll become more confident yet increasingly humble, realizing, in truth, we all have so much more to learn.

Provide help

Superheroes have amazing powers beyond the abilities of normal humans. But part of the reason they are so popular is how they emulate what we know we *can* do on our own level. We can come to the aid and assistance of others. We can activate our own powers, simply by stepping into an ordinary moment in an elevated, helpful way.

When you help someone, you create Positive Chaos. This may be as simple as holding the door open for a stranger or lifting luggage into the overhead bin for a fellow airplane passenger. You could mow a neighbor's lawn, mentor a new team member, or volunteer in your community.

Acts of assistance, small and large, begin with empathy (I seek to understand you) and progress to commitment (I am here to help you). Rather than seeing the world as an obstacle course to navigate or a puzzle to solve for your own benefit, actively seek opportunities to be of service. You can do this in three ways:

1 **See the need.** Be on the lookout for people and situations that could benefit from your assistance.

2 **Step in.** Thoughtfully offer your help without expecting or asking for anything in return.

3 **Follow through.** Once you're engaged, seek to make a lasting impact. Solve the problem if you can, or at least see it through to a significant improvement.

From the beginning of my speaking career, I sought to improve my ability to genuinely help. Over time, I advanced to new and larger opportunities by referral and recommendation. Because I delivered as promised, providing value, I was trusted, introduced to others, and asked to contribute again. It's a simple but effective business model: do great work, and you don't have to look hard for more of it.

But you cannot accept every initiation or address all worthy causes, so fielding invitations and requests requires that you develop the important skill of discernment: Where will I make the greatest impact? What is worthy and congruent? What is the opportunity cost of saying yes?

Express appreciation and gratitude

Intentional, positive, congruent action puts you on the path of elevated living. You attract the company of others who approach life with higher standards. You become like Neo in the Matrix, moving within the confines of the code, yet aware that there is so much more happening than most people realize. The tricky part, however, is staying there.

How do you maintain this new view and active engagement, even as you face your own challenges? When fatigue sets in or discouragement strikes, how do you prevent being sucked back into the psyche of mediocrity and ordinary existence? The answer is appreciation and gratitude.

Appreciation happens in the moment, capturing beauty, gratefulness, and abundance in the flow of activity and interaction. Gratitude is a deeper sense that stems from appreciation, often a reflective look back upon what happened. Appreciation is the daily response, while gratitude is the overarching condition we seek to embody.

Gratitude is astonishingly powerful. It can equally transform hardship or joy into a divine experience. It simultaneously gives strength while imbuing humility. Like plugging into a secret source, you bypass self-serving or self-limiting thoughts and move directly to a place of power. By recognizing it's not about you, you become more fully present and capable.

Many people who have spiritual beliefs regard gratitude as an essential practice. We are grateful to God and give thanks every day for both the blessings and hardships of life. We ask for humility and strength, and seek not our own glory, but the continued blessing of an active relationship with our Creator.

In a secular sense, appreciation and gratitude are also important, for what's been done on your behalf and for that which you see as worthy and valuable. Have you adequately acknowledged and thanked the people in your life?

None of us, regardless of our abilities or determined effort, achieves anything entirely on our own. The chaos of uncertainty and randomness puts people in our path who can and will help us in ways both small and enormous. Even when assistance is freely offered, without any expectation, it requires appreciation and acknowledgment. Expressing your gratitude to teachers, mentors, family members, customers, and strangers, as a regular practice, keeps you in the flow of continued Positive Chaos to come.

As an observer in life, you will see how others handle their circumstances and choices. Some of these scenes will disappoint or anger you. Many will seem ordinary and commonplace. Sometimes, you'll see how someone handles their life, job, or circumstances, and it will inspire you. When that happens, go out of your way to express your appreciation. I do this on airplanes when I see a flight attendant handle a difficult situation or complaining customer with grace and dignity. I go out of my way to, discreetly, tell that person how much I appreciate them and how they handled the situation. I don't generally do it in a public way, but more in a personal way to say, "I saw that. I learned from it. I appreciate you." Expressing appreciation to people for how they live, love, parent, work, create, and care for themselves and others serves to further positive intentions all around.

Give greater

If you want to participate more fully in the flow of abundance, go first.

"It's impossible to give more than you receive" is an important principle for my family. I still believe it to be true. Yet, I'll confess my tendency and repetitive pattern is to be generous while securing what I have, prioritizing my own needs, and hedging my bets for personal gain. I justify this by thinking, "Well, if I have more, I'll use it in a responsible way, and ultimately for the benefit of others."

My wife, Shay, however, takes a different approach. She leads with generosity. Where there is a need, she is quick to respond, without a second thought to the contrary. Once, while I was out of town on a speaking engagement, she gave away my car, telling me later, "They needed it. You can get a new one. It's a win-win." I often joked with her, "Honey, you're so giving, I'll be amazed if you get out of this life with both kidneys." We laughed about that several times, until the day we got Bob's email.

Bob Comeans is a friend of my mom's, and they worked together for several years. His son Connor was born with deformed kidneys. As a young child, Connor received a transplant from his mother, and that kidney was now rapidly failing due to accidental damage during a biopsy. At the age of seventeen, he was seriously debilitated, facing the prospect of ongoing dialysis and a highly compromised quality of life. So, Bob wrote a beautiful email speaking of Connor's life and spirit, his dreams for the future, the love and hope they shared as a family, and their desperate need at this moment for a willing donor. He sent the email to everyone he knew, including my wife and me. At this point, Shay and Connor had met exactly once.

When I got home from the office Shay approached me and asked, "Did you get Bob's email?" We held the moment, and I read the expression on her face, replying, "You're going to do it, aren't you?" Her answer was simply, "I have two." That was the extent of her thought process before she undertook to donate a body part! I don't say that to diminish my wife's analytical abilities, which are profound, but to convey how amazing she is! Generosity is her super-power, and once she made the decision, she never wavered.

I'll never forget the moment, sitting with Shay's mom in the waiting room at Emory University Hospital where Shay's kidney was removed, when I received Bob's text: "Your wife's gift just arrived for Connor." This meant her surgery had been successful, and her kidney had been transported between hospitals, through an underground tunnel, and was about to be implanted in Connor's body. Suddenly, the reality and magnitude of the moment finally hit me, and I was overcome with emotion.

To this point, we've been speaking of the amplification of small inputs to significant future outputs. To Shay, this was an easy decision, but there was nothing small about it. This was a massive act of selfless generosity offered without any expectation. I can personally attest the Positive Chaos that ensued was breathtaking.

First, of course, our family drew closer in support of Shay's decision. We also became deeply connected with the Comeans family. Connor continues to thrive twelve years later and is engaged to be married. Shay and Karen (Connor's mom) call each other "kidney sisters," as they each donated to Connor.

Additionally, I believe at least in part as a consequence of Shay's giving, our family *received* more than we could imagine, starting with large quantities of food from friends and neighbors. This was also the year we were invited to travel to Australia and South Africa for speaking engagements. Shay and I rafted the length of the Grand Canyon on the Colorado River, experiencing the adventure of a lifetime with dear friends and family. I was inducted into the Speaker Hall of Fame that year and invited to join Speakers Roundtable, the most prestigious mastermind group of my profession. We took the kids on a trip to Thailand, where I spoke for an amazing audience of eight thousand achievers. Beyond these notable highlights, however, was something far more profound—an elevated purpose and flow to life. We continued to ride what felt like a reciprocal benefit of Shay's heroic decision and actions.

When life's random requests meet your purposeful intentions, you are required to respond. We cannot all donate body parts. However, if you can give greater than you otherwise might have, you will realize Positive Chaos that will benefit or transform your life. Here are some principles to consider.

1 **Operate from abundance.** Instead of focusing on your lack of resources (money, time, energy), start with the premise that you have much to give.

2 **Open up to opportunity.** Become willing to give something greater than you may have in the past.

3 **Answer the call.** When presented an opportunity to stretch your generosity, don't hit the snooze button. Align your intentions to your actions and respond to affirm.

4 **Enjoy the ride.** Proceed without expectations and see where your generosity may take you.

Exude love and kindness

Love isn't elusive. It's immersive. It's everywhere, and it's the most powerful force on the planet. Plug into it, constantly, to align your intentions, activate your greatest gifts, and disrupt your world in the most positive way possible.

> **"Not all of us can do great things.**
>
> **But we can do small things with great love."**
>
> Mother Teresa

Just as generosity creates abundance, your capacity to experience and extend love continuously expands with use. This is, after all, the foundational element of faith, morality, and virtue. The Golden Rule: do unto others as you would have them do unto you. Love one another.

Love happens in outward ways, and through direct expression. It's also always inside you. Your essence and being will vibrate with a certain frequency that is sensed and experienced by others. Foundationally, on a sensory level, who you are and what motivates you precedes your words and actions.

When you are operating with love, your frequency will be one of calm and comfort, even when facing calamity and confrontation. You will act and speak with kindness. This isn't to say you become a pushover, subjugating your opinions to everyone else. You can be strong and firm in your opinions while being kind and loving. In fact, doing so enhances your perspective, as it conveys you genuinely care.

First, decide that a loving nature is a desired component of your journey. Understand this intellectually, then hold the intention in your heart. Realize it's easy to love those you respect, agree with, and care deeply about. But the real test and growth opportunity comes from learning to love those who are nothing like you.

In our closest relationships, love can be intimate and deeply personal. We express love with precise words, actions, and commitments.

Not once, but often, and forever. Nurturing loving relationships is like breathing, in that you're never really done. Well, until you're *done*.

Also, love is something you can exude to everyone, all the time. You project love as a field of energy, even as you drive in crowded traffic, or walk through a crowd of strangers. Smile, project love, all the time, to the best of your current ability, which will continue to grow.

WITHOUT A DOUBT, people you know and care about are experiencing immense negative chaos and suffering difficult consequences of conflict, fear, and confusion. When you activate your positive influence, you disrupt negativity for good. You create openings for new possibilities and better solutions. You become a leader. Now, let's take your leadership to a whole new level.

16

Leading Through Chaos

"I T WAS the hardest thing I ever had to do," said Matthew Whelan, president and CEO of W Services Group, when he spoke about laying off employees during COVID. W Services provides cleaning, management, and construction services for multisite retail and manufacturing facilities. When the world shut down, there was no work, no revenue, and even receivables came to a halt.

"We held on as long as we could before laying off close to fifty people"—a significant percentage of the 268 employees. "I poured my heart out to those people, kept in touch with them, made sure they and their families were safe and healthy, and they were able to apply for unemployment. We continued to treat them as part of the family, intending all along to hire them back."

Matthew's philosophy is that there is no such thing as overcommunication. At this moment of crisis—with the future of the business in the balance—he talked to everyone, constantly. They produced videos regularly, explaining in detail what they knew, didn't know, and were learning and doing to move forward. He also listened deeply, as the company's core values are to care, listen, respect, and trust one another.

"About a week before we knew we would have funding, we started hiring people back, and actually invested heavily in the relaunch."

Anticipating that the company's services—especially cleaning and safety management—would be in much higher demand during a pandemic, they doubled down on readiness, marketing, and commitment to mission. "Coming out of it, we were a stronger company and healthier team. People were even more loyal because they got to see our values in action. They had confidence in where we were going as a company, and they knew we valued them, personally."

LEADERSHIP IS like a shadow. When you seek it, or strive to protect it, it eludes you, distracts you, and requires you turn away from the light of opportunity. However, when you face the source of illumination, the shadow you cast dances behind you in perfect sync, beckoning others to follow. In this chapter I will help you realize your power to lead others through the negative chaos that frightens them while creating Positive Chaos that provides clarity and benefit.

In this metaphor, light refers to radiance of values, mission, and noble cause. It involves a commitment to honesty, integrity, and other essential human virtues. Illumination also takes the form of spiritual truth and conviction, a concentrated commitment to serve others, or the passion to achieve greater excellence individually and together. As Ellen McCarthy, CEO of Truth in Media Cooperative said, "It takes leadership to help people understand that within chaos is a wealth of opportunity."

I can tell you, without exception, that every time I encounter an outstanding culture that shares a commitment to higher ideals and aspirations, it is for one reason alone: it starts at the top. Upon experiencing a unique and extraordinary corporate culture, invariably I soon hear the statements from team members such as, "We are this way because of her spirit, encouragement, and life example," or, "Our culture is an extension of our founder. We work as hard as we do and care so much about our customers and each other because we want to be more like him."

When leaders live their values distinctively, they communicate ideas such as these:

- This is what I demand of myself and what I desire or expect from you.

- Watch me to learn what is right, worthwhile, and fun. See the spirit of curiosity and play at work in my character.

- Join us by contributing your energy and actions to meaningful work. You are important and valued.

Inspiring leaders of companies, teams, and families project belief and help others become braver and more invested in what they do. This is not just about leading by example, although that aspect is essential; this is about leading from the core of who you are. What qualities are you exuding? Do they inspire or benefit others?

During chaotic times, grounded leaders bring stability and clarity to simplify complexity. Sadly, the ability to lead others through chaos is a skill set that is severely lacking in our workforce. Of that fact our *Impact of Chaos* research was definitively clear:

81 percent of working Americans think being able to handle chaos well should be a requirement for senior leaders.

Impact of Chaos study

Also, somewhat shockingly,

70 percent of working Americans would rather make 10 percent less working for a boss who managed chaos well than make 10 percent more working for a boss who caused increasing, negative chaos.

Impact of Chaos study

This second statistic is astonishing, especially considering that *financial chaos* topped the list of highest impacting chaos types, across all demographics. As this study was conducted, Americans were experiencing rapidly increasing inflation, gas prices, and food costs. Yet, they still were willing, by overwhelming majority, to take a pay cut in order to work for an effective and confident leader.

Where in your own life would you turn to for examples of authentic leadership in chaotic times? Would it be to family members, government officials, champions of sport and business, or successful entrepreneurs and CEOs? Later in this chapter you will read the stories of several such individuals, and I hope that their responses will inform your own. Before we get there, however, let's look at why leading through chaos is so challenging.

The Complex Environment

Leading through chaos is especially difficult due to two undeniable factors:

1 Ever-increasing complexity

2 Demand for answers and certainties in an environment where they don't necessarily exist

As the global chief development officer of Chipotle Mexican Grill, Tabassum Zalotrawala is responsible for building approximately two hundred restaurants per year: securing real estate, managing construction, and maintaining high standards and tight timelines in an increasingly complex and challenging environment. She loves what she does, and she prides herself on grit, integrity, and the ability to find a way to get things done.

"I'm not just building two hundred restaurants, which could be uninspiring to think about. We're making it possible for thirty-five new employees to join our organization, multiplied two hundred times. Making it possible for families to have legitimate earnings and quality lives, and making it possible for all those communities to get access to really good food." Her belief is, no matter how complex things get, there is always a way forward.

Great leaders keep it simple. In an environment where everything is loud, important, and overwhelming, they point to the one thing that matters most. They emphasize values and reinforce intentions. Further, they spread the mission through their daily actions, constantly reminding others: *This* is what we do. And *this* is why we do it.

Great leaders use principles as primary tools for decision-making. They don't retrofit the culture to fit the chosen path. Mission, vision, and values run the show because strong, authentic leaders see themselves duty bound to serve them.

This doesn't make complexity go away, but it does provide clarity. Through a purpose-focused lens, it's easier for leaders to discern the important or essential from the noise and distractions. When you can't do everything, or understand the entire, constantly shifting picture, you can handle what you know and value with great care and integrity. You can also prioritize the care and development of your team above what could become the burden of unceasing, important work.

In Chapter 5 I told you about JP Guilbault, CEO of Navigate360. That story was an example of a leader understanding that necessary complexity was a huge factor in solving multidimensional problems. The mission of Navigate360 is to empower people, schools, and communities to stay safe and thrive physically, socially, and emotionally.

In environments where teachers, administration, and students face academic standards, plus increasing threats to safety, school shootings, a rising teen suicide rate, and immense social challenges, the team members of Navigate360 have a truly noble cause and a complex challenge. Some would even say it is insurmountable. However, that's not the way JP and his senior leaders see it. They are committed to making an enormous positive impact while creating a great place to work. Focusing on the holistic health and the wellness of the team is absolutely imperative to these results.

The nature of the work and challenges can be both a power source (purpose) and power drain (emotionally taxing and disturbing) for the employees of Navigate360. Because of that, every employee is gifted a family subscription to the Calm app, as well as instructions on how to use its guided meditations, relaxation tools, sleep soundtracks, and educational resources to promote positive mental health. They conduct monthly group sessions, which, according to chief human resources officer Alex Teodosio, are extremely popular among employees and their families.

JP also strongly advocates that team members limit their exposure to traumatic events, either at work, through the news, or in any movies and entertainment they choose to absorb, to a daily maximum of four hours. Counseling and other resources are available to help employees manage the psychological difficulties of their jobs. As a result of this holistic, values-based approach and compelling mission, turnover is low, engagement is high, and Navigate360 is consistently ranked among the top places to work. According to JP, "participating in the caring of one another is something employees highly value."

Answering in Uncertainty

The problem with leading through uncertainty is that you cannot answer all the questions. Leaders who operate from a place of fear or with a lack of confidence will often pretend they know more than they do. When faced with a question that stumps them, they may hedge their answer and offer the "safe response" that they feel will protect their air of control and play best to the room.

These kind of play-it-safe answers, however, ring hollow. People are quick to spot half-truths, safe responses, and falsehoods. They are looking for transparency in their leaders, and anything less erodes trust and confidence. In response, inquisitive employees may ask more probing questions, but most people will keep their doubts to themselves and simply modify their opinions and actions. This can result in a team that is less trusting in the leader and less willing to contribute.

Authentic leaders admit when they don't have all the answers, or when they don't have a high degree of certainty. Some leaders cannot imagine telling their people, "We really don't know exactly how this will play out," or "We still have a lot to learn about that," or "The ultimate outcome is outside of our control, but we are trying to anticipate and be ready." Ironically, our research study shows that leaders who project false or premature certainty damage their credibility. Those who are humble, honest, and real with their team engender considerable respect and confidence.

When she joined Chipotle, Tabassum Zalotrawala recalled that "for the first thirty days I was basically saying, 'I don't understand' and 'Could you please explain this to me?' The logic and processes were unfamiliar, and I was saying, 'I don't get it.' But to me, vulnerability is strength, and that resulted in the most important open rapport I have because I took the time to learn things at a foundational level."

Compounding the issues of increasing complexity and uncertainty is the reality of a decreasing, ever-tightening labor market. Some fear these workers, post-COVID, are simply not coming back to work. My view, however, is that this reality comes down to other factors including inertia, new priorities, and recalculation.

The Great Recalculation

Nearly every one of my clients is facing the same challenge, regardless of industry. Above even difficulties involving inflation, cost of goods, supply chain disruptions, and competition, people problems take precedence. When companies are short-staffed, organizations are unable to meet customer demands or even maintain regular hours at retail businesses. Business leaders are finding it difficult to hire, keep, and motivate a labor force. "People just don't want to work," they tell me. Or people are finding it hard to accept a daily commute and office assignment after extended periods of working from home.

As I've watched and continue to see this scenario play out across all industries, there is something bigger happening than simply a desire to quit. Rather than a Great Resignation, this scenario is a Great Recalculation that people are making about what is meaningful, important, and worthwhile to them.

The theory of the Great Resignation points to a notion that millions of people have left their jobs or lost their jobs and decided to remain outside the workforce. This movement seems to be led by millennials and Gen Z, starting pre-pandemic and escalating in the spring of 2021. The trend seems to be continuing in full force, with 4.5 million Americans quitting their jobs in March 2022. There are more jobs than willing or skilled workers. Because of this, workers, particularly highly qualified, dedicated workers, have additional leverage to negotiate the terms of employment.

When the world went on pause during the COVID pandemic, many people's lives and patterns were interrupted completely, and work routines came to a screeching halt or shifted into entirely new and different forms. But this pause also offered people a valuable opportunity to reexamine their lives and relationship to work. Today, in the wake of the pandemic, both employers and employees are asking new questions, either out loud or in the quiet of their own thoughts.

From the employees' perspective, these are the questions that are top of mind:

- Does my job still matter to me?

- What are the trade-offs?

- How has life changed?

- What's really important?

- Does my employer care about me?

- Is this job healthy and sustainable, and for how long?

- Does this work matter in the world?

- Can I grow, thrive, choose, and succeed?

- When I look back at my work life, will I be satisfied and proud or will I be regretful?

And here are the concerns from the perspective of the employer:

- How do we maintain and elevate our culture during times of change, growth, or increased complexity?

- Where does this culture live? In a building? On our website? In our people?

- Do you have to drive (commute to work) to be driven?

- Do we need people in offices, at home, or a hybrid solution?

- How connected do we need to be so that we can still be highly productive?

- Are we establishing precedents? Is what we agree to and accommodate now difficult to undo or withdraw?

- What will it take to get and keep the best talent and the highest quality and performance?

- How do we best collaborate and build relationships?

As these questions are being asked and answered, a new calculation is at work. Stay with me, as I will present a model that leaders can use to articulate what matters and also attain agreement with their employees in a fair trade of value.

Work-Life Alignment

I've been saying for years that the concept of work-life balance is an unattainable fallacy. This was revealed in vivid clarity when, during the pandemic, all aspects of life were suddenly compressed into uncertain reality. It's not about balance. Happiness is entirely about alignment. Think about it. Even the phrase *work-life balance* implies your work isn't technically part of your life, which is ridiculous. Your work is an extension of your life. Work is where most people spend the majority of their waking hours and gain financial fuel that satisfies basic needs and enables opportunities. Work can be an outlet for unique expression, satisfying accomplishment, and artistic contribution. At its best, work is an investment and deep involvement in what is meaningful and worthwhile.

In my view, the equation is not work versus life, but work aligned with life.

If business leaders can see corporate missions and the opportunities afforded by employment as a means for others to realize their personal best, then they can unlock greater synergy between strengths, talents, and contributions.

How do you want people to engage with their job? Does your current work environment create the expectations and conditions where each of these four components exists?

WORK: Willingness, Ownership, Responsibility, Knowledge

I am **Willing** to do what it takes and requires. Willing to learn and grow.

I take **Ownership** of outcomes. My choice. My job. My culture and values. My mistakes and successes.

I am **Responsible**. I am dependable, reliable, and able to respond with speed and effectiveness, regardless of my physical location.

I have the **Knowledge**. I know what to do and how to do it. I know I matter and am valued. I know my work and company serve a meaningful mission.

If you can't get good people to work for you, stay with you, or push themselves to deliver, the issue may be that what you expect and offer to them is out of alignment with what is acceptable and enticing. But the answer isn't just about financial compensation. That's part of it, sure. Financial chaos is consistently the primary source of anxiety and stress. But the issue is bigger than that.

As a business leader, what is your organization offering to people in terms of clear communication, culture, and opportunities to learn and grow? Are your purpose and values distinct and enticing? Are you clear about what you expect, both in terms of responsibilities and adherence to principles? Are you willing to enable your people to find creative ways to deliver the outcomes you desire?

Consider how these mutual commitments could constitute a new agreement between employers and employees.

The New Agreement of Fair Trade

EMPLOYER	EMPLOYEE
Clear communication	Clearly communicates
Leads with values	Cocreates the culture
Invested in your life	Committed to learn and grow
Open to new approaches	Owns their outcomes
Provides compelling purpose	Believes in the cause
Dynamic compensation	Commitment and adaptability

Effective communication must be mutual. Employers convey clear requirements, expectations, and timely information. Employees agree to ask questions and share ideas and challenges they are experiencing. In this way, the communication flows freely, problems get addressed more quickly, and people learn from one another.

Growth goes both ways. Employers must see themselves as net contributors to their employees' lives. This contribution goes beyond offering a paycheck and extends to promoting mental and physical health, family and relationship dynamics, and overall well-being. Employees can commit to pursuing growth and improvement and sharing and celebrating one another's breakthroughs.

Purpose isn't imposed and followed. It is embodied and shared. The organizational mission and values are constantly reinforced and referenced in personal and professional examples by leaders and employees alike.

Unfolding innovation. While providing clear expectations of requirements, employers remain open to new approaches, allowing their people to innovate, provided they own (meet or exceed) agreed upon outcomes.

Exchanging value. Compensation takes more dynamic forms, including money, benefits, flex time, and learning and life-enhancing opportunities. In exchange, employees pledge commitment and agree to adapt to changing circumstances.

The Core Competencies

Now that you have some sense of the real-time challenges, thought, and agreements that are required to build an effective team in the midst of chaos, let's speak more specifically to the competencies and behaviors of an effective leader.

First, let me break down each of the top four attributes that our study determined to be the essential qualities of effective leaders during times of chaos. Remember that leaders with these abilities are so highly valued that 70 percent of working Americans would prefer to make 10 percent less and work for such a leader than make 10 percent more reporting to a boss who lacked them. If you are a business leader, entrepreneur, or manager, or want to lead your family and friends, the following are the competencies you need to be effective.

Clear communication

By far, this was the most important of the characteristics in terms of ranked value. During times of chaos, you cannot presume others understand what you do. These are the actions that ensure your communication is clear:

- share information and updates with greater frequency.

- conduct individual and group listening sessions to take in others' ideas and perspectives.

- invite contributions from those who wouldn't normally get a chance to speak.

- set the expectation that everyone has a valued perspective which deserves to be heard.

- when in "listening mode," ask probing questions, and restate what you learn to convey that you hear and understand the message.

Adaptability

Leading through chaos requires you demonstrate you can make real-time adjustments. The ability to adapt and incorporate new information doesn't make you wishy-washy—it makes you nimble and discerning. You need not incorporate everything or change course as a reflexive response. This quality is discernment. When you demonstrate some adaptability in certain aspects while resisting changes and adjustments in other areas, you establish you are flexible yet *committed to principles*. This is key. Don't compromise or adapt your values, principles, or mission as you flex. Instead, use values and principles to evaluate new pathways, then adjust your approach to elevate what continues to matter most.

Decisiveness

Dr. Nido Qubein is the president of High Point University, an astonishingly successful, rapidly expanding, award-winning regional university in High Point, North Carolina. Since Nido took the helm in 2005, HPU has had the riveted attention of the world of education. They do things differently, disrupting traditional patterns every day. The transformation continues and accelerates each year, with new academic schools, beautiful buildings, and an entirely new approach to advanced education—teaching higher learning *and* higher living.

An enormous component of the success story is Nido's unparalleled decisiveness. He once told me, "You never get all the information you'd like before you decide. If you're lucky, you get maybe 75 to 80 percent of the information. Yet you have to be the one to step up and say, 'This is it. We're going this way.'" In the world of education, nobody has been able to make bigger, faster decisions than Nido. As a result of his incredible clarity of purpose, values, and vision, HPU continues to rise in prominence and success every year while other, established universities face unprecedented challenges.

During times of chaos, you don't have the luxury of delaying decisions. You will need to make tough choices while adhering to your principles and leading with your values. When you know and do the right thing, it may be the more difficult choice. But to an authentic leader, it is the necessary choice and the only real option. You will get pushback, but if you've done your job of listening and communicating, you've earned the right to decide. Own the decision and the consequences. Once you make a decision, don't second-guess it. You will never know the outcome of the choices not taken, as you've just instantly invoked the irreversibility principle (Chapter 4). Go all in and create more Positive Chaos to come.

Transparency

When you lead with the truth, you instantly win respect. You connect with humility. You stand in the confidence of saying, "Here's what's happening, for better and for worse; this is what we know so far. Let me show you what's working and wonderful, as well as what is troubling and difficult."

Steer clear of blame and judgment and simply share the unfettered reality of what is happening. Honestly, that's all people want to know. They're thinking, "Just tell me what's going on. I can take it!" If you don't give them a complete story, they will fill in missing details with their own presumptions. Generally, when the missing details are authored by other people, they won't project the highest hopes or best intentions as these so-called details are the product of a fearful mindset. Get in front of falsehoods or, when you can't, defuse them with truth. Remain approachable, accessible, and willing to answer questions. In this way, you'll embody undeniable, authentic leadership.

What Authentic Leadership Looks Like

According to our study, the top four qualities of effective leadership through chaos were, in order of importance: clear communication (46 percent), willingness to adapt or adjust quickly (38 percent), problem-solving or decision-making (38 percent), and being honest and candid (33 percent).

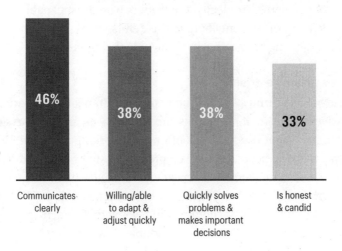

WHAT ARE THE CHARACTERISTICS OF A LEADER WHO HANDLES CHAOS WELL?

(by total and ranked; respondents were allowed to select multiple characteristics)

46%

38%

38%

33%

Communicates clearly

Willing/able to adapt & adjust quickly

Quickly solves problems & makes important decisions

Is honest & candid

Notice that the top four most valued attributes of leadership are not about being right. They are all about being real, honest, adaptable, willing to share what's unknown, and still find a way forward.

Here's how that plays into the behaviors of authentic leaders.

Embraces vulnerability

Effective leaders model the example of lifelong learning. This means they are willing to get things wrong and own their mistakes. Rather than revealing weakness, this vulnerable quality exhibits strength and conveys congruence. This is not to say leaders should divulge the entirety of their weaknesses or doubts. It is necessary to maintain strength of authority and command in the midst of chaos. However, an effective leader must be committed to owning the truth of the circumstances, especially when that truth reveals an opportunity for learning, correction, or improvement. In this regard, humility and ownership convey confidence and willingness to learn, grow, and accept help.

The opposite of this is the leader who pretends they know more than everyone else or is unwilling to admit an obvious error or deficiency. Everybody knows it, and they discuss it privately; however, the boss is unable or unwilling to admit it. They mask incompetence with frantic activity, unproductive meetings, and complex attempts to solve problems. Ironically, the leaders who are incapable of vulnerable truth often contribute to the demise of plans and projects while projecting blame on what is outside their control.

Never wastes a crisis

During chaotic times people and teams simultaneously experience massive change, multiple options, mixed messages, and obvious signs of decline. What used to work often isn't working anymore. What wasn't working becomes an even greater waste of time and effort.

These fearful conditions reveal extraordinary opportunities for the authentic leader—a license to try something new. With the mindset of uncertainty—not knowing, yet actively participating in the unfolding story—leaders can double down on mission, leverage the unique qualities of team members, and encourage elevated curiosity and communication. The notion here is: We are building something new, necessary, and extraordinary. We don't exactly know what it is yet, and we are discovering it together. This means we must communicate, sharing our excitement, ideas, and learning in real time. We also must be brave enough to let go of what we know isn't working.

Great leaders, including Tabassum Zalotrawala, encourage over-communication. "When chaos hits, be transparent. It's okay to tell your people, 'I'm not sure. Stick with me. Let's tell each other everything and figure this out together.'" Rather than coming across as micro-managing, this approach fosters an environment of macro-learning. Everyone learns something valuable. By sharing real-time understanding and breakthroughs, you get to the innovative solution much faster than if you are all trying to work it out alone.

Creates space for change

Many individuals and teams are unwilling to abandon the behaviors, systems, and patterns they know aren't working because they are familiar. I call this phenomenon the false premise of *dysfunctional permanence*. The thinking is, "Until and unless we find a better replacement, we must keep doing something. So, we'll keep doing what we know and are good at (even though it doesn't work)."

The problem of not changing until you have the next answer is analogous to believing that you can't stop banging your head against the wall until you get a better idea. But the high probability is you won't get a better idea until and unless you stop pounding your head into the wall—quite the catch-22! Yet this concept of dysfunctional permanence is pervasive in people and teams everywhere. Often, the better answer is only accessible once you stop what you're doing, creating the space to change. Then, at this point, the next, better plan, path, or answer may become obvious.

Remember, all you ever get is some certainty, and the future is both unknowable and unfolding. The authentic leader steps into this reality with the courage to create space for change. In this way, they foster excitement while empowering others to create meaningful new possibilities.

Releases what isn't working

Steve Jobs, cofounder of Apple, was famous for his reality distortion field. People who worked with him described this phenomenon. First, they encountered what appeared to be an unsolvable problem and certain failure. Then, Jobs would interact with them, and his belief was so powerful that he transcended the doubt and caused others to solve "impossible" problems simply because they must be solved. This is a rare gift, a combination of relentless drive, audacity, arrogance, genius, and obstinance.

Some modern-day leaders, such as Elon Musk, also possess some of these characteristics and the rare ability to warp reality to solve the "impossible." With SpaceX, Musk commercialized "affordable" satellite launches by inventing entirely new systems, designs, and reusable rockets that returned to Earth, landing, as in a sci-fi movie, as gracefully as they launched. But the cost was extraordinary: SpaceX spent billions of dollars and blew up many tons of rockets. Musk has an enormous willingness and capacity to invest and take risks in order to accelerate learning, develop ability, and achieve success. And remember, SpaceX's satellite business is a stepping stone for the larger goals of manned launches to the Moon (coming soon) and, eventually, Mars. With each new system and milestone, spectacular (unmanned) explosions are acceptable costs, as they teach the greatest lessons.

Still, the notion that any vision or intention, once imagined, planned, and articulated, will inevitably become realized is … well … untrue. The idea that "if you can envision it, you can attain it" has led countless people and organizations to pursue wrongheaded plans and projects, ignoring obvious impediments and evidence while exhausting enormous resources of time, money, and effort. Even when leaders bring passion and clarity of vision, certainty of the path forward, and unwavering commitment to just keep going and make this thing happen—it doesn't always make that thing happen.

Many goals are not attained. I'd even venture to say most are not. This may be due to lack of willingness, desire, ability, capacity, or achievability on the part of the organizational leadership and the team members. Your determinism must play in the phase space of *others'* determinism (that of competitors, regulators, detractors, customers, employees, even of the world, with its ever-shifting conditions). There's also randomness to contend with, which can work against you or in your favor. Even if you see others pulling off what you envision, it does not necessarily mean it is within the realm of your capability.

While we can understand the power of belief and determination to inspire and enable those around us (as we talked about in the previous chapter, about influence), most of us mere mortals are better served with a sense of realistic optimism. As you lead your teams, it's wise to measure your unbridled confidence and encouragement with accurate assessments of reality and truthful reminders that success is still undetermined. Just because it should be doesn't mean it will be.

Everything comes at a cost. There are times that the most courageous move a leader can make is to release a goal or intention that is obviously outside the realm of possibility, or that is far more costly (in time, money, talent, or opportunity) than it's worth.

LEADERSHIP DURING times of chaos requires more of you. Often more effort. However, sheer force or unbending will are, themselves, insufficient. Leading through chaos requires more curiosity, more empathy, more communication, more transparency, more vulnerability, and more courage. Yet these asks do not have to be onerous. They can be liberating, freeing you to discover and pursue opportunities that were never available until this very moment. Seize the opportunity with clarity and conviction, and you will create Positive Chaos for those you lead and serve.

MORE CHAOS
TO COME

WHETHER OR NOT you are leading an organization, a team, a cause, or a family, you are, most definitely, leading your life. Among those who know you well and those who know you slightly, you convey a sense of hope or fear. Confidence or helplessness. Joy or anxiety. Please lead your life with great conviction, as there is, no doubt, more chaos to come.

I wrote this book with you in mind. I care deeply about your well-being and know you are capable of great things, and great love. Engage with the chaos you face—the waves of disruption—by simplifying complexity, finding synergy, and consistently choosing a more positive polarity and higher-level pattern.

Stay calm in calamity, find truth in transition, and pursue peace in the process of perpetual change. Use the mindsets and skill sets you've learned to sidestep senselessness and shake up your world. Have fun creating positive disruptions, then watch, with curious excitement, what happens when you do. Not only will you experience chaos differently, rising above negative emotions like anxiety, hopelessness, and pessimism, but you'll also see better options and act with confidence and clarity of intention. When you apply what you've learned, life gets better and you simultaneously release control of some outcomes while realizing profound abilities to shape your world.

Be patient. Remember, transformation can happen in an instant, yet the timelines often take longer than you'd like. And remember this too: Your most important project is your health. Nothing you touch gets significantly better until you do. Take charge of your physical and mental well-being; improve your ability to improve yourself.

As the chaos of the world continues to increase, be affirmed: you have new understanding and transformed abilities to respond with intention. As the battles intensify between hope and fear, right and wrong, good and evil, and love and hate, choose hope, right, good, and love. Help others as you guard yourself, maintaining precious momentum, an upward trajectory, and ever-increasing alignment with what truly matters.

ACKNOWLEDGMENTS

'M CONVINCED books don't want to be finished. This book is no exception. What you hold in your hand now is a testament to determination and the result of many individuals' contributions to slaying (or perhaps caging) the metaphorical dragon. I wish to acknowledge the contributions of many special people to this project.

First, I'd like to thank my family for providing stability while contributing beautiful complexity. Our great kids, Eddie and Maggie, always make me smile while helping me see things differently. Shay, my wife, is a wonderful creative partner in life and business and affords me the space to write, play, travel, and speak (while basically keeping our lives running). To my parents and sisters for their life-long influence, inspiration, and support, I am also forever grateful.

Thanks to Stephanie Craig, my longtime assistant and event coordinator, for expertly managing all the moving parts, flights, and shipped cases, for reminding me what's next, ensuring I hit my deadlines, and always pointing me in the right direction.

To the amazing men of my mastermind group—Tim Gard, Mike Rayburn, Waldo Waldman, Chad Hymas, and Daniel Burrus—my immense gratitude for your many years of friendship, assistance, inspiration, and accountability in life and business. A special thank-you to Daniel for writing the foreword and contributing poignant insights, as always. I'm also immensely grateful for the support and examples of my fellow members of Speakers Roundtable.

I'd like to thank Jason Dorsey, Jared Boucher, and the team at the Center for Generational Kinetics for helping us design and execute a world-class research study resulting in profound, important, and (at times) disturbing discoveries about the impact of chaos on the American workforce. Thanks to JP Guilbault, Ellen McCarthy, Monica Rothgery, Chris Stites, Matthew Whelan, and Tabassum Zalotrawala for contributing valuable stories and insights to me and the reader.

I'd like to acknowledge and thank Trena, Adrineh, Sarah, Rachel, Chris, Taysia, and everyone at Page Two for elevating every aspect of *Positive Chaos*. And thank you to Phil Jones for making the introduction and sharing his favorite book partner with me.

Thanks to Shep Hyken for introducing me to the National Speakers Association (and so many other opportunities), quite literally changing the course of my life. To NSA, I owe enormous gratitude for providing the pathway to discovering my dream vocation, my highest contributions, and innumerable amazing, cherished friends.

And finally, a heartfelt and massive thank you goes out to *all* the clients, corporations, associations, agents, bureau partners, production companies, and individuals who have continued to provide new invitations and opportunities for me to do what I love and am meant to do in the service of helping others.

NOTES

Introduction

p. 5   Impact of Chaos in the American Workforce *study*... Dan Thurmon, *Impact of Chaos in the American Workforce: Key Findings Revealing the Current State and Impact of Chaos on Workers and Leaders and Suggested Strategies to Improve Wellbeing and Performance* (Motivation Works, Inc.; study conducted in partnership with the Center for Generational Kinetics, 2022), available at danthurmon.com/research.

Chapter 1: Testing Positive

p. 18   *"Do you truly know what is positive and what is negative?*... Eckhart Tolle, *The Power of Now: A Guide to Spiritual Enlightenment* (Novato, CA: New World Library, 2004), 177.

Chapter 3: Butterfly Effectiveness

p. 56   *"An intellect which at any given moment*... Ali Bulent Çambel, *Applied Chaos Theory: A Paradigm for Complexity* (St. Louis: Elsevier, 1992), 7.

p. 56   *Other groundbreaking discoveries*... Çambel, *Applied Chaos Theory*, 35–36.

Chapter 5: Complexity Simplified

p. 85   *A 2019 Harvard Business Review article*... Anthony Dukes and Yi Zhu, "Why Is Customer Service So Bad? Because It's Profitable," *Harvard Business Review*, February 8, 2019, hbr.org/2019/02/why-is-customer-service-so-bad-because-its-profitable.

Chapter 7: The Price of Positive

p. 104   *in 2022, both print media and television media* ... Jeffrey M. Jones, "Confidence in U.S. Institutions Down; Average at New Low," Gallup, July 5, 2022, news.gallup.com/poll/394283/confidence-institutions-down-average-new-low.aspx.

Chapter 9: Transformation 2: From Hectic to Healthy

p. 145   *According to the Centers for Disease Control and Prevention, obesity* ... "Health Effects of Overweight and Obesity," Centers for Disease Control and Prevention, last reviewed September 24, 2022, cdc.gov/healthyweight/effects/index.html.

p. 145   *a prevalence for population obesity above 35 percent* ... See "Adult Obesity Is Increasing," Centers for Disease Control and Prevention, last reviewed September 27, 2022, cdc.gov/obesity/data/obesity-and-covid-19.html#Increasing.

p. 145   *The number of annual deaths attributable to obesity* ... David B. Allison, Kevin R. Fontaine, JoAnn E. Manson, June Stevens, and Theodore B. VanItallie, "Annual Deaths Attributable to Obesity in the United States," *Journal of the American Medical Association* 282, no. 16 (1999): 1530–38, doi.org/10.1001/jama.282.16.1530.

Chapter 10: Transformation 3: From Anxious to Aspiring

p. 149   *it's your frontal cortex that won't let it go* ... Elizabeth I. Martin, Kerry J. Ressler, Elisabeth Binder, and Charles B. Nemeroff, "The Neurobiology of Anxiety Disorders: Brain Imaging, Genetics, and Psychoneuroendocrinology," *Psychiatric Clinics of North America* 32, no. 3 (September 2009): 549–75, doi.org/10.1016/j.psc.2009.05.004; "The Science of Anxiety (Infographic)," Northwestern Medicine, June 2020, nm.org/healthbeat/healthy-tips/emotional-health/the-science-of-anxiety; Neil M. Dundon, Allison D. Shapiro, Viktoriya Babenko, Gold N. Okafor, and Scott T. Grafton, "Ventromedial Prefrontal Cortex Activity and Sympathetic Allostasis During Value-Based Ambivalence," *Frontiers in Behavioral Neuroscience* 22 (February 2021), doi.org/10.3389/fnbeh.2021.615796.

p. 149   *more than 25 percent increase in cases of anxiety and depression* ... COVID-19 Mental Disorders Collaborators, "Global Prevalence and Burden of Depressive and Anxiety Disorders in 204 Countries and Territories in 2020 Due to the COVID-19 Pandemic," *The Lancet* 398, no. 10312 (November 6, 2021): 1700–12, doi.org/10.1016/S0140-6736(21)02143-7.

p. 150   *37 percent of Gen Z "tech natives" believed technology weakened their inter-personal skills* ... Anna Wolfe, "37% of Gen Z Say Tech Has Weakened

Their People Skills," Hospitality Technology, July 26, 2018, hospitality tech.com/37-gen-z-say-tech-has-weakened-their-people-skills.

p. 153 *Today more people are educated and fewer are in poverty...* Peter Diamandis, "Data... World Getting Better," *Peter H. Diamandis* (blog), June 25, 2016, diamandis.com/blog/data-world-getting-better.

p. 153 *Cancer death rates have fallen every year...* ACS Medical Content and News Staff, "Risk of Dying from Cancer Continues to Drop at an Accelerated Pace," American Cancer Society, January 12, 2022, cancer .org/latest-news/facts-and-figures-2022.html#:~:text=The%20risk%20 of%20death%20from,to%20a%20world%20without%20cancer.

Chapter 14: New Metrics—Gains Beyond Goals

p. 204 *"should commit itself to achieving the goal...* John F. Kennedy, "Address to Joint Session of Congress," John F. Kennedy Presidential Library and Museum, May 25, 1961, jfklibrary.org/node/16986.

p. 205 *"Life List" of 127 extraordinary objectives...* John Goddard, "Life List," *John Goddard* (blog), johngoddard.info/life_list.htm.

Chapter 15: Incredible Influence and Positive Disruption

p. 222 *"Social media influencer" is, according to research...* Daniyal Malik, "Research Proves 'Influencer' as One of the Most Popular Career Options Among Children," Digital Information World, February 3, 2019, digitalinformationworld.com/2019/02/young-affiliates-children-aspire-to-be-social-media-influencers-youtubers.html.

p. 223 *In 2022, a study found that 45 percent of Gen Z creators...* Jo Constanz, "Gen Z Wants to Ditch Corporate Jobs for Influencing, Social Media Dreams," *Bloomberg*, August 25, 2022, bloomberg.com/news/ articles/2022-08-25/gen-z-wants-careers-as-influencers-content-creators-but-have-to-go-all-in.

Chapter 16: Leading Through Chaos

p. 244 *The theory of the Great Resignation...* Joseph Fuller and William Kerr, "The Great Resignation Didn't Start with the Pandemic," *Harvard Business Review*, March 23, 2022, hbr.org/2022/03/ the-great-resignation-didnt-start-with-the-pandemic; Derek Thompson, "Three Myths of the Great Resignation," *The Atlantic*, December 8, 2021, theatlantic.com/ideas/archive/2021/12/ great-resignation-myths-quitting-jobs/620927.

p. 244 *4.5 million Americans quitting their jobs in March 2022...* Anneken Tappe, "A Record 4.5 Million Americans Quit Their Jobs in March," CNN Business, May 3, 2022, cnn.com/2022/05/03/economy/job-openings-quits-march/index.html.

INDEX

(eustress), 179, 181; recharacterization of, 181; reframing trauma, 178–79
synergy: autonomous growth (silos), 185; in business, 184–85; life design for, 182–84, *183*; long term pursuit, 185–87; patterns of, 187; positive complexity, 184; Steamboat ski resort, 175–76

Teodosio, Alex, 242
Thurmon, Dan: *Off Balance On Purpose*, 9, 84, 182
Thurmon, Eddie, 132
Thurmon, Maggie, 22–23, 61–62
Thurmon, Shay, 181, 232–34
Truth in Media Cooperative, 103–4

Vondruska, Mike, 53–54, 159, 206

W Services Group, 237
WAC Model, *39*, *41*; ability, 36, 36–38; assess your WAC (exercises), 43;

capacity, 38–41, *39*; success in uncertainty, 42; willingness (*See* willingness)
Weihenmayer, Erik, 116–17; *No Barriers*, 117
Whelan, Matthew, 237–38
"Why Is Customer Service So Bad? Because It's Profitable" (*Harvard Business Review*), 85
willingness, *29*; amplify upside, 31; behavior modification, 32; clarify downside, 31; empathic leadership, 32–33; foundation of effort, 36; limitations of, 35–36; motivation, 32, 33–34; ownership, 30; spectacularly pretending, 34, 107
Workforce Preparedness Study (McDonald's), 150

Zalotrawala, Tabassum, 111, 240–41, 243, 253

YOU NEVER KNOW
WHO'S IN YOUR AUDIENCE

THIS MOTTO has helped me fuel my mission and strive for excellence while staying ever present to this undeniable reality: *Wherever you go, there are people who need help and opportunities to deepen connections while expanding impact.*

Usually, you don't know who might be hurting and needs encouragement most, or where your next amazing friend may come from. And you never know the full measure of how you influence others.

With that in mind, please know I would genuinely love to hear from you.

Visit **danthurmon.com** to reach out with inquires or stories, including any of the following:

- **Share how this book or my presentations impacted you and your team**. I always love to hear these stories—and I love it even more when they're shared on review sites of your favorite online retailers (if you do this, you get bonus points!).

- **Convey your ideas about collaborating to deliver a powerful keynote** for your company or association's conference. Whether it's by setting the theme and energy as an opening speaker, providing the "call to action" closing keynote, or something in between, I'd love to help you accomplish your meeting goals.

- **Explore executive coaching and group masterminds.** Perhaps you'd rather dive into a deeper conversation about how I can help you and your team implement the concepts of this book or achieve new breakthroughs.

- **Make a request to purchase the book in bulk.** Get your entire team "on the same page," literally! I can even combine your give-away with a virtual event where I deliver key concepts and answer questions.

Additionally, you can follow me on social media:
🔗 📷 @danthurmon

If this book helped you, please share it with someone you care about. Give them your copy. Or, better yet, keep yours and buy them their very own. Let's spread Positive Chaos together.

Wherever you go and whatever you do, remember little things change everything, and the world needs you in a very big way.

Your fan,

DAN

ABOUT
THE AUTHOR

DAN THURMON has delivered thousands of presentations across six continents for audiences including world leaders, Fortune 500 companies, entrepreneurs, educators, and even troops on the front lines of battle. His unique presentations incorporate powerful messages, amazing displays of acrobatics, and audience interaction to create powerful learning experiences. Dan is the author of *Off Balance On Purpose* and has produced, together with his son, Eddie, over four hundred videos in a popular weekly coaching series for clients and followers. Additionally, Dan has served as president of the National Speakers Association and has been inducted into the prestigious Speaker Hall of Fame. Dan is also well known on social media, enjoying, along with his daughter, Maggie, many millions of followers, and hundreds of millions of views of their video content featuring hilarious and heartwarming father-daughter fun. Currently, Dan lives in the Atlanta area with his life and business partner, Shay, and their two dogs, Simon and Spencer.